YUNUS EMRE
The Sufi Poet in Love

Zekeriya Başkal

BLUE DOME

13 12 11 10 1 2 3 4

Published by Blue Dome Press
244 Fifth Avenue #2HS
New York, NY 10001

www.bluedomepress.com

Library of Congress Cataloging-in-Publication Data Available

ISBN: 978-1-935295-05-1

Printed by
Çağlayan A.Ş., İzmir - Turkey

CONTENTS

FOREWORD

The commemoration by UNESCO in 1991 of the 750th anniversary of the birth of the Anatolian Sufi poet, Yunus Emre (ca. 1241–1321) and in 2007 of the 800th anniversary of the birth of another Anatolian Sufi poet, Rumi (1207–1273), has brought increased international acclaim to both of these celebrated figures. Yet rarely has Yunus Emre been considered in terms of the Islamic civilizational context he shared with Rumi in an era when Muslim thinkers of the stature of Ibn Arabi (1165–1240) and Fakhruddin Iraqi (1213–1289) were drawn to the intellectual and artistic centers of Seljukid Anatolia. Both within Turkey and without, Yunus Emre has been portrayed as an unlettered poet of love whose vibrant poems lived across the centuries in the oral traditions of the unsophisticated. In the present work, Zekeriya Başkal seeks to rectify this limited understanding which thwarts easy recognition of Rumi and Yunus as figures who shared the same philosophical and cultural environment, but used different languages, Persian and Turkish, and different genres of poetry, *mesnevi* (or *mathnawi*, poems composed in rhyming couplets) and *ilahi* (devotional hymn), to express their message.

Granted, the affinity of these two great poets has been stressed in the past. In a brief essay Ahmet Hamdi Tanpınar (1901–1962), the prominent intellectual, poet and novelist takes as a given "the closeness in sensibility and mentality of Yunus to his renowned contemporary Rumi," but holds that this intellectual closeness cannot diminish the distinctiveness that sets Yunus apart as poet of unique singularity. (*Edebiyat Üzerine Makaleler*, 1969 p. 141). Speaking in more general terms, the well-known scholar of Islamic mysticism, Annemarie Schimmel (1922–2003) has pointed out that: "In the case of Yunus Emre, one cannot possibly deny the orthodox Islamic foundation of all his thought, although some modern Turkish interpreters are inclined to forget the Islamic roots of his poetry. The Qur'an is for him the basis of all wisdom." (Halman, ed. 1981 p. 65). Nevertheless, there continues to be a disinclination to link Rumi and Yunus and a tendency to lift Yunus out of his Muslim context altogether.

Zekeriya Başkal addresses this situation by drawing on recent developments in reception and reader response theory to propose a series of explanations. He provides an analytic overview of the most prominent interpreters and schools of interpretation that have characterized the reception of Yunus Emre's poetry in the 20th century, while presenting evidence from across the centuries that Yunus Emre had a place not only in the oral tradition, but also among important segments of the Ottoman elites, including composers, poets, and the writers of philosophical commentaries. Furthermore, Başkal indicates that Yunus Emre was embraced as an exemplary figure by a diversity of Sufi orders and that appreciation of his poetry and its spiritual message was not exclusive to the Bektashi order of dervishes. All of this is set in the context of the historical and social conditions of Anatolia in which the Seljukid centers of learning continued to flourish, despite the devastations following the Mongol-Ilkhanid victory at Kösedağ in 1243. Most importantly, Başkal takes into account Yunus Emre's poetic output in its entirety and demonstrates that its dominant themes require analysis in terms of the philosophical concepts of Islamic mysticism that were current in the centers of learning of his day. Thus, Başkal's analysis, which takes as a basic resource the 1990 critical edition by Mustafa Tatçı, is consonant with Ahmet Hamdi Tanpınar's much earlier estimation that the individual poems of Yunus "...which relate the mystical system with all of its subtleties and his *Risale-i Nushiyye* (allegorical treatise) itself, which was one of the important works of his period, show us in clarity a truly exceptional mind and superior intellectuality nourished on all the knowledge of his time." Tanpınar continues his thought by stating, "However, the faculty of mind and intellect was not Yunus' dominant quality. He was before all else a man of the heart. He was one of those who found human fortune within himself in all its pain and sublimeness." (*Edebiyat Üzerine Makaleler*, 1969 p. 141). It would be virtually impossible to find anyone, regardless of interpretive framework, who would disagree with this latter part of Tanpınar's estimation, even if they were to disregard or fail to comprehend the former. Ultimately, it may prove to be that Yunus Emre will remain what readers choose to make of him, as they relate to the power and beauty of his poems. We are fortunate, however, to have available the present work, which for the first time locates Yunus Emre in his own historical and cultural context, while providing an informative and insightful analysis of the multiplicity of competing modes in the interpretation of his poetry, a first step perhaps towards a reconciliation of them.

Sarah G. Moment Atis
Professor of Turkish
University of Wisconsin-Madison

INTRODUCTION

Yunus Emre (c.1240–c.1320) is one of the most famous poets in the history of Turkish literature. His poems have been quoted, recited, and sung in a number of different environments, from novels to daily columns, political discussions and Sufi circles. With the translations of his works into English, French, German, Urdu, as well as many other languages, and with the celebration of 1991 as the year of Yunus Emre by UNESCO, Yunus Emre has become well known as a Sufi saint-poet who exerted a great influence in both the East and the West.[1] The ardent, deceptively simple, yet powerful expressions of love, the musicality of the verse, and the daring and sometimes even daunting imagery are among the features of his poetry which attract people from various walks of life. From 1918 on many works in the 20th century have been devoted to Yunus Emre. The works of Fuat Köprülü (1890–1966), Abdülbaki Gölpınarlı (1900–1982), Burhan Toprak (1906–1967), Talat S. Halman (b. 1931) and finally Mustafa Tatçı (b. 1961) are milestones in Yunus Emre scholarship. Other than these major contributions, there have been hundreds of articles and a number of books that discuss the personality and poetry of Yunus Emre.[2]

However, these works have not been able to rid themselves of certain defects for two main reasons: the lack of a comprehensive critical edition of the work of Yunus Emre prior to 1990 and, more importantly, the ideological motivations of some scholars who considered the study of Yunus Emre to be an arena for developing political agendas, rather than an area of scholarship in its own right.

In the present work, I will demonstrate how in much of the previous scholarship the poetry of Yunus Emre was utilized to construct the authors' own version of a distant history, and even their own version of contemporary history, and the future. I will analyze both critical and popular works on Yunus Emre, and provide an alternative approach. Without trying to prove any preconceived assumptions about Yunus Emre and by relying, for the most part, on textual materials, I will attempt to place Yunus Emre and his poetry within their historical and textual context. I will compare what the authors who wrote on Yunus Emre have said about his poetry with the information that is available from primary sources.

There are some problems that have prevented the scholars and authors who are writing about Yunus Emre from reaching definitive conclusions on issues regarding the poet himself, such as the lack of specific biographical information. A more important problem, however, is pertinent to the approaches to the poetry of Yunus Emre. There are several ideological approaches to his works; the most prevalent of these are imagining a Turkish past in the 14th century for the sake of contemporary Turkish nationalism, Orientalist approaches, for example considering Yunus Emre to be a Christ-like person who could not have drawn his inspiration from Muslim sources, apologetic approaches that present Yunus Emre as a pacifist in an effort to deconstruct the image of the terrible Turk—particularly in the West—and finally, what I call "the springboard approach", which uses the poetry of Yunus Emre as a springboard from which to attack certain issues, such as Ottoman culture, Muslim history, etc. I will demonstrate how these approaches take their references from the audience to which they are addressed or from issues that remain mostly outside the poetry of Yunus Emre, demonstrating how they conform to or differ from Yunus Emre's body of poetry.

In Chapter 1, I will provide information about the social, political, and intellectual environment of Yunus Emre. I will argue that Yunus Emre inherited a rich and complex cultural legacy from the final period of the Seljukid state, rather than from volatile and unstable times that had limited cultural and economic resources; it will also be demonstrated how this is reflected in his poetry. I will discuss the importance of Sufism at the time, and identify the major brotherhoods in order to locate Yunus Emre within his own historical and intellectual context.

In Chapter 2, I will discuss the function of poetry in the 13th and 14th centuries, which is essential in terms of interpreting the poetry of Yunus Emre, as the function inherently affects the composition process, as well as the interpretation. I will also provide an example of the interpretation of his poems based on the contemporaraneous Sufi understanding by referring to Ibn Arabi, who is an important link in a long chain of major figures that includes Mevlana Jalaluddin Rumi (1207–1273) and Fakhruddin Iraqi (1213–1289). I will also discuss the language of Yunus Emre, an important element both in his poetry and in his reception. I will discuss language not simply from the aspect of the linguistic origins of the words, but as a system of signs that carry a set of cultural values.

In Chapter 3, a theoretical framework for the reception of Yunus Emre in the modern period will be presented. The approach that I have utilized does not grant a definitive conclusion for the issues discussed; rather, it provides alternative perspectives and concepts. The constructivist role of literary history discussed by scholars such as Hans Robert Jauss has proven to be relevant in clarifying the complexity of issues that underlie the desire of diverse groups to claim Yunus Emre as their own. Although I did not set out to achieve this goal at the beginning of the work, by the end I had realized that some of the approaches to the poetry of Yunus Emre could easily be judged to be a disservice to the literary history of modern Turkish society at the expense of the textual and historical material. The issue of whether Yunus Emre was a Bektashi or not and the historical development of the Bektashi order, as presented in works on Yunus Emre by various scholars, will be discussed and interpreted within the framework of how literary works can play a constructive role without compromising textual and historical veracity.

In Chapter 3 I will also demonstrate that the poetry of Yunus Emre was well appreciated among various classes in the Ottoman period, thereby dispelling one of the major arguments in Yunus Emre scholarship which asserts that only a very limited segment of Sufis and people in rural areas appreciated his poetry. I will use written and oral sources, poetic parallels (*nazira*), commentaries (*sharh*), and musical performance to demonstrate the widespread appreciation of Yunus Emre. In the section "Reception of Yunus Emre in the Modern Period" I will demonstrate that the prevalent modes of understanding the poetry of Yunus Emre do not correspond with the textual or historical materials. I have divided the reception of Yunus Emre into four categories: nationalist, heterodox, humanist, and individual interpretations. In the last category I have included arguments that cannot be considered to be a school of interpretation, but which are very important nonetheless due to the stature of the scholars who advanced them.

I have used the works of Köprülü, Gölpınarlı, and Tatçı as my main references. Gölpınarlı, in spite of holding problematic and sometimes contradictory views on Yunus Emre, nonetheless provides reliable and significant information for understanding the reception of Yunus Emre in the Ottoman period. The 1990 critical edition of the *Divan*[3] of Yunus Emre, which Mustafa Tatçı produced after comparing more than ten versions of the manuscript, was also an indispensable source for this study.

Note on Transliteration

In this work, the Turkish names of people and their written works, as well as place-names within the boundaries of Turkey, have been transcribed according to official Turkish orthography. Accordingly, *c* is read as *j*, *ç* is *ch*, *ş* is *sh*, the *ğ* is silent, but lengthens the preceding vowel, *ı* is pronounced like the "o" in "atom," *ö* is the same as the German letter in Köln or the French "eu" as in "peu," and finally *ü* is the same as the German letter in Düsseldorf or the French "u" in "lune."

ACKNOWLEDGMENTS

The origins of this book date back to my PhD dissertation at the University of Wisconsin-Madison. I was fortunate to have a wonderful circle of teachers and friends during my five years at the university. I would like to express my sincerely grateful feelings for Professor Sarah G. Moment Atiş, who was not only my dissertation advisor but also an excellent teacher, and who gave me new perspectives on many issues, including my own culture and country. Professor Atiş spent many hours helping me to mold this work into its current form. Professor Kemal Karpat read the work and made useful suggestions in the earlier stages of the dissertation. Professor Uli Schamiloglu was kind enough to read every single page at least twice, sharing his deep interest, broad knowledge and encouraging enthusiasm. Professor Muhammad Umar Memon pointed out the cross cultural elements in Yunus Emre and encouraged me "to think outside the box."

I was again fortunate to have a wonderful circle of friends who always offered their support. Jessica E. McAbee, Tevfik Koşar, John Holevoet, Dr. Ali Emre Özyıldırım, Dr. Hüseyin Özcan, Hrag Varjabadian, Scott Randall, John Bragg, and Walter Slater helped in various ways and edited the rough edges of the writing with many excellent suggestions. I should also thank my dear wife Ayşe Mungan, who gave so much and who convinced me once again that the contributions and intelligence of the "other half" of humanity do matter.

I would also like to thank Dr. Mustafa Tatçı, who has so enriched my understanding of Yunus Emre. He was always generous with assistance, be it his ideas on Yunus Emre, newly published books in the field, or the birth date of a poet from the 19th century. I should not forget Professor Ramazan Kaplan, who encouraged me to work in this field. The Ministry of National Education of Turkey and Department of Languages and Cultures of Asia at University of Wisconsin-Madison have provided me with the funding that enabled me to complete my studies.

My thanks to Hüseyin Bingül and Jane Louise Kandur for their editorial expertise and guidance and to Blue Dome Press who have made this publication possible.

I am sure that there are mistakes and unexplored areas in this work. Needless to say, all the shortcomings are mine.

Zekeriya Başkal
Tokat, October 2009

Chapter 1

The Age in Which Yunus Emre Lived and His Place in the Sufi Tradition of His Time

THE AGE IN WHICH YUNUS EMRE LIVED AND HIS PLACE IN THE SUFI TRADITION OF HIS TIME

The Social Context of the 13th and 14th Centuries

In order to fully understand the poetry of Yunus Emre, one has to consider the social, political, and cultural conditions of his time. More importantly, one must take into account the conditions of the era before Yunus Emre, which dated back to the period of the Anatolian Seljukid state and provided him with a rich cultural heritage. Although there is controversy over exactly when Yunus Emre lived, it is generally accepted that he was born around 1240 and died around 1320, at approximately eighty years of age. This means that he lived between the decline of the Anatolian Seljukid state and the beginning of the Ottoman state. This period is commonly referred to as the period of *Beylik*s (Turkish Anatolian Principalities). Many modern scholars have depicted the *Beylik* period as one of chaos, instability, and warlike conditions and have portrayed Yunus Emre as a product of this period.[1] However, when one considers the culture and conditions of the earlier period, it becomes clear that the poetry of Yunus Emre was more a culmination of this last period of the Seljukid state rather than of the period in which he lived. Although Yunus Emre lived during the *Beylik* period, he inherited the cultural legacy of the previous period, one that represents an apogee in the history of Anatolia in terms of both culture and economy. This cultural legacy had very little to do with the political events of the era in which Yunus Emre lived. As Claude Cahen puts it, "...intellectual life in Anatolia after 1243 represents the full flowering of a process which had first begun in the time of the last Seljukids."[2]

While it is true that the Mongols did much damage to the Anatolian Seljukid state, culture, and society in Anatolia, this damage was only a temporary and regional phenomenon which abated over time. Eventually, the Mongols adopted the religion and mores of the societies they had defeated; in some cases, such as that of the Ilkhanids,[3] the Mongols even supported cultural activities to a greater degree than they had in their previous lands.[4] The way the Mongol commanders treated prominent scholars, such as Mevlana Jalaluddin Rumi (1207–1273) and Fakhruddin Iraqi (1213–1289) is a clear example of this behavior.[5] No doubt, a centralized power and an organized state were very important for the development of art and other cultural activities. The guild-like *akhi* organizations, about which more information will be given later, and the system of patronage prevented a total disruption of the stability of the region in which Yunus Emre grew up and composed his poetry.[6] Over time, due to various political and cultural reasons, including the fact that the Mongol invasion of Central Asia and the Iranian plateau caused many scholars to move westwards and settle in Anatolia, this region became a center for learning and science. The fact that Anatolia was also part of the larger Seljukid state caused Anatolian soil to become an incredibly fertile field for cultural development.

An Overview of the Seljukid Period

After the victory of the Seljuk Turks against the Byzantine army at Manzikert in 1071 the doors of Anatolia were opened to them. Soon after this event, one of the great grandsons of Selçuk, Süleyman Şah, took control of İznik in northwestern Turkey and Konya in central Turkey (1078) and established the Anatolian Seljukid state. Accompanying the Seljukid army, Turkmen people from Central Asia advanced westward along various routes. After the death of Süleyman Şah, his son, Kılıçarslan (1091–1107), became sultan of the Anatolian Seljukid state. When Kılıçarslan surrounded

Malatya to the southeast, the first Crusaders invaded İznik in the northwest, returning it to Byzantium.

After moving the capital from İznik to Konya, Kılıçarslan established order in Anatolia and tried to develop commercial life, succeeding to a degree. His death in 1107 ended this order; the Byzantines in the west and the Armenians in the south continually attacked the Anatolian Seljukid State. After a long struggle between the two sons of Kılıçarslan, Mesud became the sultan in 1116. During his long sultanate, Mesud conquered the Kastamonu region in northern Anatolia and the Maraş region in the south. It was only with great difficulty that Mesud was able to prevent the invasion of Konya by the Byzantine forces. Willing to take advantage of this weakness, the Byzantine state prepared an army of 100,000 soldiers to expel the Turks from Anatolia once and for all. However, the son of Sultan Mesud, İzzettin Kılıçarslan, defeated the Byzantine army in Miryekefelon in 1176. This victory marked the end of Byzantium's hopes for expelling the Turks, who until then had been regarded as invaders of Anatolia. Another outcome of this victory was that the trade routes for the Mediterranean and Black Sea were secured and the Seljukid borders reached the Aegean Sea. Soon after, the Seljukids took over Alanya and Antalya, two very important ports for world trade, particularly for the Venetians. Later on, the Seljukids also took over the ports of Sinop in the north and Sugdaq in the Crimea. With all of these victories, Anatolia became the homeland of the Turks, who were eventually to become the founders and the main element of Ottoman society.

Towards the end of his life, İzzettin Kılıçarslan divided the country among his sons. This raised tension among the brothers and caused instability in the country. In 1190, the Second Crusader army, which had set out as a result of Salahaddin's conquest of Jerusalem (1187), invaded Konya, the capital of the Anatolian Seljukids; they destroyed the city and killed its population. However, after the Crusaders left Alaaddin Keykaus was able to establish order; at this time, between 1200 and 1240, the Anatolian Seljukid state was at the apex of its power.

During this period, Alaaddin Keykaus (1211–1219) and his son Alaaddin Keykubat (1220–1237) signed peace treaties with the Byzantine state; these treaties proved mostly effective. It was during this period of peace that the Anatolian Seljukid state tried to stabilize its eastern and southern borders with the Armenians and the Syrians, and with the Byzantines to the north in Trabzon. At this time, the Anatolian Seljukid state "…was one of the great powers in the Orient [and] the undisputed master of the whole of Anatolia from the coast opposite Rhodes to the sources of the Tigris and from Dorylaion to Mount Ararat…"[7] This golden age came to an end for the Seljukid state due to an internal problem, the rebellion of Baba İshak (d.1240) in 1240. Baba İshak, who it was believed could make contact with the occult, gathered Turkmens, mostly from the countryside, claiming that he was a prophet of God. The false prophet and his followers rebelled against the Seljukid state; the state was able to defeat them only with great difficulty thanks to the help of the soldiers from the neighboring Christian lords, who did not believe in Baba İshak's alleged supernatural powers. By this time the Anatolian Seljukid state had become neighbors with the Khwarezmshah state and the Mongols to the east. The Mongols and the Seljukid armies met in Kösedağ, near Sivas in central Anatolia; here Keyhusrev II was defeated by Bayju Noyan, the Mongol commander, in 1243.

After this defeat, the Anatolian Seljukid state became a vassal of the Mongols and had to pay heavy taxes. With the death of Keyhusrev II, the country descended into a series of internal struggles. In 1261, Rükneddin Keykaus reestablished order. However, the real power was in the hand of Vizier Pervane Muineddin Süleyman, who tried very hard to be an intermediary not only between the Mongols and the Seljukids, but also between the Mongols who were coming to Anatolia and the settled Turkmens. After the death of Pervane, Seljukid sultans in Konya lost their quasi-independence and took orders directly from the Mongol administration. During this time we see various Anatolian Turkish principalities (*beyliks*), such as the Karamanoğuları (1250?–1475?), Germiyanoğulları (1260–1429), and Çandaroğulları (1291–1461), attempting to maintain order and become dominant in the region. At this time, power was predominantly exercised by these principalities and Ilkhanids. The other prevalent phenomenon of this period in terms of politics was the Mongol expeditions into Anatolia, which attempted to implement order and punish those who had rebelled against the Mongols or who had ignored tax payments. The death of Alaaddin Keykubat III in 1308 is generally accepted as the end of the Anatolian Seljukid state. After this date, we see the Ottomans in Anatolia, first as a regional power, and then as a world power.

It is commonly accepted that the Anatolian Seljukid state, as part of the Muslim east, had a great number of similarities with the other Muslim states of the time, despite local differences and the pre-Islamic past of the Turks. Although there are different opinions on this matter, they are mostly related to nationalist, Orientalist apologetical, or other forms of ideological historiography.[8] The main attribute of the Anatolian Seljukid state in terms of religious life was that most of the population adhered to the Sunni interpretation of Islam and followed the Hanafi legal school of thought and practice, although there were Shafiis, too.[9] Some scholars even consider the Seljukids to have been the leading factor in preventing Shiite thought from becoming a major component in the Islamic world, or at least in delaying the role that Shiite thought was to play.[10] The Seljukids inherited a great deal of scholarship that was developed in Khorasan, Transoxania and the centers of the Abbasid caliphate. In the deliverance of this inheritance, the contributions made by scholars who came to Anatolia not only to avoid the Mongol invasion, but also because they were attracted by the large number of learning centers, the prosperity and the tolerant conditions, are undeniable.[11]

In the thirteenth century, Anatolia was an international meeting place for science, Sufism, and trade. No doubt the Mongol invasion played a role in some scholars arriving in, or rather, fleeing to, Anatolia. However, the main reasons for such an influx were Anatolia's rich cultural and materially prosperous centers, such as Konya, the Seljukid capital, and Tokat, Sivas, Malatya, and Kayseri. In these centers scholars were treated with a great respect by both the locals and the rulers. Furthermore, scholars were provided with every possible means to teach and spread their messages. Fakhruddin Iraqi (d.1289), who was born in Hamadan, Iran, traveled throughout the Islamic world and eventually settled in Anatolia for the reasons mentioned above. Even during the time of the Mongol invasion, he received a great deal of respect from both the Seljukid rulers, such as the famous Seljukid vizier Muineddin Pervane, and Mongol commanders.[12] Among the scholars who came to Anatolia we can also count Bahauddin Walad, the father of Jalaluddin Rumi (1151–1231), Jalaluddin Rumi (1207–1273), Ibn Arabi (1165–1240), and Najmuddin Daya (d.1256), who composed his *Mirsad* in Sivas in 1230.[13]

Starting in the 13th century, the number of *madrasa*s increased rapidly in the major centers of the Seljukid state. Along with the *madrasa*s, the dervish lodges, another institution of religious life, flourished at the height of Seljukid power. Konya, Sivas, Malatya, Tokat, and Kayseri became centers for Sufi learning and practice. From various sources and architectural remains it is safe to say that there were *kulliya*s (complex of buildings) with Sufi hospices, schools, hospitals, and kitchens in every part of the country.[14]

This period is also the time in which major Sufi orders, such as the Mevlevis [also Mawlawis], Bektashis, Qalandaris, Malamatis, Khalwatis, Kubrawis, and Rifa'is, were established or became widespread in Anatolia. The founder of the Mevlevi order, which is also known as the Whirling Dervishes, was Sultan Walad, the son of Rumi, who lived in Konya; the main figure of the Bektashi order, although the order was formed later, was Hacı Bektaş, who also lived in Kırşehir in Central Anatolia, while the founder of the Kubrawiyya, Najmuddin Kubra (1158–1221), also lived in Konya.[15]

Rumi, still a well-known name, is a good representative of this period in terms of synthesizing and reflecting the major movements. Since there are plenty of sources concerned with him and there is a strong similarity between Rumi and Yunus Emre in many respects, discussing the main elements of Rumi's life can shed light on the period of Yunus Emre. There is a strong possibility that these two met, and it is a fact that Yunus Emre was familiar with Rumi and his works.[16] Rumi came to Anatolia from Khorasan when he was very young and settled in Konya, the capital of the Anatolian Seljukid state. The decision to settle in Konya was made after Keykubat invited Rumi's father to come. Rumi represents three important socio-religious movements. The first is the strict Sunni *madrasa* education. This movement is represented by his background and his father and first teacher, Bahauddin Walad. It is known that Rumi was a professor of law and that he acknowledged his father's influence on him. The second movement, which can be called the theoretical aspect of Sufism, is represented by Ibn Arabi (1165–1240), who was a Muslim of Andalusian origin. This movement had a tremendous influence throughout the Muslim world. Ibn Arabi developed the idea of the unity of being as a system, and he was the author of many famous books, such as *Futuhat al-Makkiyya* (The Meccan Openings), *Fusus al-Hikam* (The Bezels of Wisdom), *Anwar* (Lights) and *Tarjuman al-Ashwaq* (The Interpreter of the Yearnings).[17] Ibn Arabi traveled to Anatolia twice and stayed there for three years, once in 1205, and again from 1216 to 1218. His disciple Arifuddin Sulayman of Tlemsen in North Africa also stayed in Anatolia for many years. When Ibn Arabi was in Anatolia he was a guest of Mejdeddin Ishak, the father of Sadreddin Konevi (d.1234), a famous Sufi. Ibn Arabi's works were widely read and many commentaries were written about them. The influence of Ibn Arabi in Anatolia was immense, both directly, as in the case of Konevi, Arifuddin Sulayman, Fakhruddin Iraqi, and Muayyuddin Jandi (d.1291), and indirectly, as in the case of Rumi, Yazıcıoğlu Mehmet (d.1451), and İbrahim Gülşehri (c. 1317). The third movement that Rumi benefited from was the Iranian Sufi School, as represented by Shams Tabrizi (d.1247), who came to Konya. It was through Tabrizi that Rumi came to understand and treasure the Sufi way of approaching knowledge and life.

In addition to Rumi and the atmosphere in the towns of Anatolia, the Turkmen holy dervishes (*dervishan-ı Rum*) were another important religious element of the period, particularly in the countryside. Both before and during the Mongol invasion, many dervishes came to Anatolia. There was a wide range of dervishes, from the very orthodox to the heterodox. Their common feature was that they spoke the language of the masses. Furthermore, they lived among the people and gained their trust because of their reputation for honesty, generosity, and wonder-working. They played a great role in the Islamization of Anatolia. Archival studies provide us with a detailed description of the exploration and rejuvenation of Anatolia by Sufis. They policed towns and insecure roads, helped to form trade guilds in the towns, opened farmlands, and introduced new technology to agricultural areas. For instance, the Sufis introduced peach cultivation to the region of Bursa, which is still famous today in Turkey for its peaches.[18] Some of them spread Shiite ideas and sometimes posed a great danger for the Seljukid state. The most famous examples of this are Baba İshak and Cimri.

Although economically there were some difficult times, particularly during the invasions of the Crusaders and the Mongols, Anatolia lived in great prosperity. There is agreement among scholars about the prosperous condition of the country during the Seljukid state. The state provided excellent conditions for merchants, and both internal and foreign trade flourished. From various textual sources and remnants of certain buildings we can tell that every 16 miles in Anatolia there was a caravanserai that linked the principal cities of the state; this was the distance of one day's march. The lives and goods of merchants were insured by the state in case of robbery, shipwreck, or any kind of damage. The Seljukids controlled the major trade routes and levied transit taxes. The caravanserai, bridges, and inns provided safe and easy transportation for merchants, and brought income for the state. Sources tell us that the income of the Seljukid state in the time of Melikşah in 1336 was incomparably more than the annual income of France or England at the time.[19]

The economic situation was not very different during the time of the Anatolian Turkish principalities. A number of scholars argue that although there was disorder and instability in the region after the decline of the Seljukid state, it was neither continuous nor present in every part of Anatolia. This period was an era of "intense commercial and cultural activity."[20] The decline of the Anatolian Seljukid state did not mean the impoverishment of the country; rather, it meant the transfer of resources either to the Ilkhanid state or to the Anatolian Turkish principalities. The number of literary works that were written and the number of *madrasa*s and major architectural works that were constructed in this period as compared to the earlier period are a clear sign of this.[21]

One of the most important types of socio-economic institutions that provided such continuity was the *akhi* organizations, that is, mystical fraternities of craftsmen.[22] The *akhi* was a kind of guild with certain social functions. It was the convergence of two elements: the first was economic, as can also be seen in other cultures, such as ancient Iran and India, and the second consisted of social and religious elements. This second aspect was originally proposed by the Abbasid caliph an-Nasirudinullah (1180–1225) to secure the unity of Islamic countries by way of creating a group called *fityan*, or *futuwwa* (youth). One of the most highly regarded Sufis, Suhrawardi (d.1234), visited the Seljukid palace in Anatolia as a part of this enterprise. *Futuwwatnama*s, which became a genre that mainly prescribed what the characteristics of a virtuous man should be, were also part of this movement, and continued to exist in the Seljukid and later Ottoman periods. Every artisan branch was organized within itself and all of the organizations were within a structure that resembled a confederation; this also had a leader. The leader of each branch and the leader of the entire confederation both had a role and a degree of influence that was very similar to the head of a religious order.

*Akhi*s not only controlled the amount and quality of products produced by their members, but also controlled their social life and internal order. In a sense, they undertook many responsibilities that could be considered to be duties of the state, such as punishing those who did not follow the rules, defending the city or region in times of war, and educating the members of the union not only in their professions, but also in other areas. When the Seljukid state lost power after the Mongol invasion, the *akhis* established a kind of local government that provided security and stability.

In terms of cultural activities, we observe the same wealth that existed in the economy. Three main languages were used in the Seljukid State: Persian was the spoken language of many intellectuals and was used by the state in chancery, while Arabic also was used in the *madrasa*s and as the language of correspondence between Muslim states; finally, Turkish was used to communicate with the Turkmen population and the army. Ibn Bibi (d.1280) tells us that the Seljukid State used notarized translators to communicate with the Christian powers of the time and their Christian subjects.

The use of various languages can be seen in the literary works of Sufi figures. Rumi used Arabic and Persian, and sometimes Turkish and Greek words to express his feelings. One anecdote by Rumi depicts the linguistic aspect of this period colorfully. One day Rumi heard a peddler passing by his house with fox skins for sale, shouting "*tilku, tilku*," which is the word for fox in Turkish. Being a Sufi and finding God in everything he heard or saw, Rumi took this as "*dil ku, dil ku*" which means in Persian "Where is the heart? Where is the heart?"[23] We see this diversity of lexical items within the Turkish language, too; for example, in Yunus Emre's poetry, there are many words from Persian and Arabic. The preference of one language over another for the Seljukids was a matter of practicality rather than an ideological tendency, although some scholars have presented it this way in retrospect.

The richness and diversity of this period in the field of literature is not really apparent in the discussions and historiography of national history. Selective historical writing has included Yunus Emre, but not Rumi, Hoca Dehhani, but not Fakhruddin Iraqi based solely on the language they used in their literary works. For someone who is not well-read in Seljukid history or who does not view history critically it would be very difficult to imagine Rumi or Yunus Emre in the same cultural environment, sharing similar values and sources, although they express them formally in different ways by using different languages. This narrow understanding is reflected not only in the history of the time, but also in the interpretation of the texts produced in this period, as shown in Chapter 3 in the section entitled "The Reception of Yunus Emre." Mehmet Bey of Karamanoğulları (d.1277) for instance, is portrayed as an important figure who helped to secure the future of the Turkish language by issuing a decree that enforced the use of Turkish in every aspect of life.

In the works that cover this period, or in the works of Yunus Emre, for that matter, Turkish literature in Anatolia begins with the son of Rumi, Sultan Walad (1226–1312), who wrote some verses in Turkish, and continues with Ahmed Fakih, Gülşehri, and Hoca Dehhani. Here, it is appropriate to examine the matter of what makes a literature Turkish or Persian. In the majority of books on this issue it is assumed that language is the primary, indeed, the only element that makes a literature Turkish or Persian.[24] When we consider the works of Yunus Emre and Rumi, we can see that the only difference is the language they used. It is almost impossible to find other major differences that would indicate important distinctions between these two men's work. The only difference between the *Mathnawi* by Rumi and *Risalatu'n Nushiyya* [or *Risale-i Nushiyye*], the work of Yunus Emre, both written in the same meter and genre, is the language used in the two works. This type of division of literature can be considered a retrospective and anachronistic understanding of history, and one that, to a great extent, carries the flaws of a twentieth-century perspective with it.

Until the period of the Anatolian Turkish principalities it is very difficult to find works written in Turkish in Anatolia. However, it is most likely that the Turkmens brought their oral traditions from Central Asia and continued to use them in Anatolia. The continuation of the troubadour (*aşık*) literature, which has many Central Asian Turkic elements, in later centuries is a clear sign of this. We see a few Turkish lines in Rumi's works and a number of Turkish verses in the works of his son. Ahmed Fakih (d.1233), who burned his books as a sign of his refusal to accept a certain type of knowledge, before going off into the mountains to live the life of an ascetic, can be considered to be the first person who composed poetry in Turkish in Anatolia. Among the pioneers were Şeyyad Hamza, the author of *Yusuf ile Züleyha*, Gülşehri from Kırşehir, who put Faridu'ddin Attar's *Mantiq at-Tayr* (The Conference of the Birds) into verse, Hoca Dehhani, who wrote both in Turkish and Persian, and Aşık Paşa (1271–1332), who wrote a didactic poem entitled *Garibname* that explained the basic elements of Sufism and defends Sunni thought. It should also be stated that with Yunus Emre the use of Turkish for poetry reached its zenith in the 14th century. We can complete the list by mentioning the name of Nasreddin Hodja, a folk figure, known as "Mulla Nasruddin" in Iran, and "Juha" in North Africa and many other places, such as Greece and Russia. He is known for his anecdotes and remembered as a witty judge, a joker, a fool, and an educator.[25]

The names and events mentioned so far are just a small portion of a greater picture. In a variety of aspects Anatolian Seljukids took and masterfully made use of the many institutions that had been developed before them. One of the defining characteristics of the history of this period was symbiosis, in the sense that the Seljukids utilized and contributed many cultural elements through an exchange of ideas with the societies that they came into contact with. It should be kept in mind that the Anatolian Seljukid state was not detached from the other Seljukids or Muslim states. They were part of a bigger cultural and political tradition, and the period of Yunus Emre also should be considered within this broader perspective.

An Introductory Overview of Sufism

It would not be an exaggeration to suggest that without understanding Sufism, no matter what kind of analytical tools are used, it is impossible to understand the poetry of Yunus Emre. This understanding will provide us with a better framework for determining the specific position of Yunus Emre within the broader context of the religious thought of his day. There are various explanations of Sufism and what terms can be used to identify this phenomenon. Some of the terms currently in use are Islamic mysticism, esotericism, Islamic spirituality, the Sufi Way, and *tasawwuf*. When looking at Islamic texts, although it is possible to see the use of the word "Sufi", even by early Muslims,[26] one cannot see the term "Sufism" in any texts except those written in the modern period. Instead, we see the term *tasawwuf* used for the discipline, and there is a set vocabulary, for example, being a *dervish* or *faqir* (poor person with the awareness of his or her poverty and helplessness before God), as well as *zawq* (spiritual pleasure), *Haqiqa Muhammadiya* (Muhammadan reality), and so on. For instance, *The Risalah* of Al-Qushayri (d.1072) is one of the early complete manuals of the discipline of *Tasawwuf*, or Sufism. Indeed, the very term Sufism, with the "ism" addition, was coined by and gained a wide usage with the British Orientalists,[27] people who were interested in differentiating certain tolerant aspects of Islam from the stricter elements, that is, the aspects that they found attractive and peaceful, rather than dogmatic. For instance, Reynold A. Nicholson mentions Sufism and Islam as independent entities and says that Sufis "make logical compromise[s] with Islam."[28] Unfortunately, the currency of this term has created an apparent duality in the present day, making it appear as if Islam and Sufism are two different and sometimes mutually exclusive or antagonistic concepts.[29]

Both in the past and the present, the term Sufism has been used in works that pertain to Islam and works by Muslims in both positive and negative ways. When this term is used in the positive sense, Sufism follows the model that was exemplified in the personality of

Prophet Muhammad, peace and blessings be upon him. When Sufism is used in a negative sense it then comes to mean *bid'ah* (innovation) and external influences that are opposed to the spirit of Islam.

Just as there are many different terms and interpretations encompassed by Sufism, there are also various explanations for the origin of the word *Sufi*. The most common explanations are that the word derives from the word for wool garment (*suf*), pure (*saf*), or that it refers to the scholarly Companions who lived in the chamber adjacent to the Mosque of the Prophet in Medina during the time of the Prophet (known as the *Ahl as-Suffa*), or from the Greek word for knowledge (*sophos*).

In this work, the word Sufi is used to denote a Muslim who is trying to realize the perfect human being in their personality as prescribed in the Qur'an and Sunnah, the way of God's Messenger, which includes every act, word, and confirmation of the Prophet. We should also bear in mind that Sufis emphasize inner development, the inner esoteric meanings of the sacred texts, and the imagination.

A hadith, known as the hadith of Gabriel,[30] which is very often used in Sufi texts, helps us to better understand the term Sufism—or the reality that is called Sufism—and its relation with other aspects of Islam. It can be summarized as follows: One day when the Prophet was sitting with the Companions, a man came and asked three questions. The Prophet answered the questions, which were: "What is Islam (submission), what is *iman* (belief) and what is *ihsan* (doing the best)?" After Prophet Muhammad, peace and blessings be upon him, had answered these questions the man left and the Prophet told the Companions that this person was Archangel Gabriel and that he had come to teach the religion to the Companions. The third aspect, *ihsan*, is what Sufism tries to accomplish.

The first question asked by Gabriel was about Islam (submission) and there are a number of explanations as to what this term refers to. The main elements of Islam are performing the obligatory ritual prayers, fasting during the month of Ramadan from dawn to dusk, visiting Mecca for pilgrimage, giving prescribed alms, and proclaiming the *shahada*, that is: "I witness that there is no god but God and Muhammad is the servant and Messenger of God." These five pillars of the religion are the aspects that are mostly concentrated on by jurists (*fuqaha*).

The second question in the hadith is concerned with *iman*, which basically can be divided into six premises. These are "to believe in the existence and oneness of God, the angels, the Divine Scriptures, the Prophets, the Last Day, and to believe in divine destiny, both the good and the evil thereof." This part of the hadith is primarily dealt with by theologians (*mutakallimun*), traditionists, namely, those who study hadiths (*muhaddith*), and interpreters of the Qur'an (*mufassirun*).

The third concept mentioned in the hadith, *ihsan* ("perfection" or "doing what is best"), is mostly examined in Sufi writings, although explanations can be found in other texts as well. The basic explanation Sufis provide for this term is that by following the example of the Prophet and by developing spiritually one can reach a point where it is possible to see things as they are in their true form. The first two elements—submission and belief—are very important in reaching this point, as they are the foundations of *ihsan*. Sufism is what the methods that help one reach this point of perfection are called. Sufism is mainly concerned with how the heart, the most important human faculty, can be purified, and how the heart as well as one's actions, thoughts, and personal consciousness can be perfected. In a way, Sufism could be called *ilm al-qulub* (the science of hearts).[31] Throughout the ages and across the far reaches of the Islamic world, various orders or brotherhoods (*tariqa*), such as the Naqshibandiya, the Chistiya, and the Mevleviya, have served as repositories for this "science" or methodology. The majority of the orders take reference from the Qur'an and the Sunna, and they accept the first two elements in the hadith as being the foundations of *ihsan*.

The Sufi understanding of the universe, humankind, and God, as well as the relationship between these, can be summarized as follows: according to Sufis, God created human beings because He wanted to be known. In this act, the most important motive was love. The well-known and often repeated hadith qudsi[32] that is found in Sufi texts states: "I was a Hidden Treasure and I loved to be known. Hence I created creatures that I might be known."[33] Hence, the reason for the existence of the universe and humans, who are the essence of the universe, is to know God (*marifah*).[34] Humans have the potential to become a being higher than the angels or lower than the animals. By following the methods explained in the Qur'an and Sunna, which were later elaborated on in the teachings of Sufi sages and teachers, one can perfect oneself by being one who knows God (an *arif*), and better attempt to reach the perfect form for which they were created (*insan al-kamil*).

In completing the final stage of *ihsan*, after submission (Islam) and belief (*iman*), there are methods and guidelines that one should follow. There are many Sufi writings that outline the steps and pitfalls that make up the path to *ihsan*. The main goal of Sufis in providing a road map for the initiate is to help the heart and the soul (self) reach perfection. In order to do this, one has to start from the soul. The soul has various forms or stages, from the lowest one, the evil commanding soul (*nafs al-ammara*), to the highest one, the soul at peace with God (*nafs al-mutmainna*). The process of eliminating the evil elements of the soul and transforming it into a better form is one of the main goals of Sufism. In order to do this one has to do two things: The first is to come to know the self by studying and examining its various aspects.* The second tool used to cultivate and purify the soul is remembrance (*dhikr*), which is considered to be an exercise of the soul.

---

* Yunus Emre expresses this idea beautifully:

> *Okumaktan maksadın kişi kendin bilmektir*
> *Sen kendini bilmezsin bu nice okumaktir*
> ("The reason for studying is to know one's self
> If you do not know yourself what good is this studying")

Yunus Emre Divanı, Mustafa Tatçı (ed.), 2 vols. (Ankara: Kültür Bakanlığı, 1990, Vol. II, p. 67).

It is no surprise that Sufism places the self in a very important position. The self is important for a number of reasons; first of all, the self reflects the attributes and signs of God in a complex and condensed way. In Sufi thought God's various signs include the universe, the Qur'an, and creatures/beings. Just like the stars, solar systems, and other creations, the verses of the Qur'an are called signs (*ayat*), as they are indications of the existence and attributes of God. Yet the self performs the same indicating role in the most perfect way. It is largely for this reason that a very common theme in Sufi literature is the use of a mirror as a metaphor for hearts and humans. Another feature that makes the human self so important is the fact that everything else indicates or shows the signs of God without any free will (*irada*); humans are the only exceptions to this. In other words, the planets have to act in a certain way and there is a predetermined route that they have to follow. Human beings, however, have the freedom to choose a variety of paths, not all of which are necessarily approved of by God.

The second reason the human self is important is the duties that human beings undertake. In the Qur'an it is stated, "*We offered the Trust (al-Amanah) to the heavens and the mountains, but they shrank from bearing it, and were afraid of it (fearful of being unable to fulfill its responsibility), but the human has undertaken it. He is indeed prone to doing great wrong and misjudging, and acting out of sheer ignorance*" (33:72). This trust means humans are able to be the representatives of God in the world by reflecting His attributes.

The second key to progressing on the path in the way of perfection is remembrance. Remembrance has various meanings, ranging from simply repeating the names of God to systematically contemplating theological issues. Various orders have developed different ways in which the initiates can practice remembrance; these methods sometimes fascinate outsiders, although they are considered to be minor or secondary issues by Sufis. The attention on the outward aspect of the *sema* performances of professional Whirling Dervishes is a good example of this lack of content. Basically, remembrance is a kind of spiritual exercise to become closer to God, to eliminate the unwanted elements in the soul, thereby purifying it. Since the goal of Sufism is to employ all the human faculties in the way of God, Sufis try every possible way permitted by the religion to reach this goal. Some of the other exercises that Sufis practice are repentance (*tawba*), self-criticism (*muhasaba*), reflection (*tafakkur*), privacy and retreat (*halwat*), self-supervision (*muraqaba*), reliance (*tawakkul*) and patience (*sabr*).[35] Although these are not well recognized or visible to outsiders, they are as important and vital as remembrance for the Sufi. Sufi sages and teachers prescribe and apply these practices in such a meticulous way that it is almost like a material being processed in a laboratory, or more aptly, the transformation of coal into a diamond, which is then polished and cut with the facets to make it into a jewel.

During the early centuries of Islam, in order to fully apply the process of self-criticism (*muhasaba*), some people either wrote down or kept in mind what they did each day in order to analyze and criticize their actions at the end of the day. Another example is the *halwat*, or retreating to a secluded place with minimum social interaction for a certain period of time. In order to think more carefully and to analyze their actions and thoughts more completely, Sufis would often live in a secluded place, eat less, particularly less of certain kinds of food, drink less, talk less, and sleep less. In an effort to internalize the transitory nature of the world and the lonely fact of death in the Naqhshibandi order, initiates would contemplate the moment of being lowered into the grave and the image of their family and friends bidding farewell and walking away from their grave.[36]

The reason why such practices were undertaken was to become close to God by becoming a perfect human being, which is, indeed, the ultimate aim of Sufism. When initiates fulfill the requirements of Sufism it is possible that they can become close to God. In an often-repeated hadith qudsi God states:

> My servant draws near to Me through nothing I love more than that which I have made obligatory for him. My servant never ceases drawing near to me through supererogatory works until I love him. Then when I love him, I am his hearing by which he hears, his sight by which he sees, his hand by which he grasps, and his foot by which he walks.[37]

People who reach this stage experience the company of God, and depending upon their style or specific order, they may express things that are difficult for others to understand, and their ecstatic outbursts may lead people to believe that they are heretics. An example of this is Hallaj al-Mansur's famous expression "I am the Truth" (*Ana'l-Haqq*). This aspect, and other aspects of Sufism, are treated in detail in the works of, in particular, Ibn Arabi and other Sufi figures such as Abd al-Karim ibn Hawazin al-Qushayri (986–1072) and Muhammad al-Ghazali (d.1111). One should approach Sufism by considering the ideas and main frameworks found in these Sufi writings, and by considering Sufism as a wide spectrum that has many different colors and appearances. It is also important to bear in mind that what we call Sufism is an aspect of Islam, a religion that has been practiced among very different societies for fourteen centuries, across the vast landscape of the Islamic world. It is only natural that there are linguistic, cultural, theological, and historical differences apparent in such a long-lasting and wide-reaching movement; at the same time, there are many unchanging elements which form the main structural bases of Sufism. As Hodgson rightly puts it, "the Sufis were reasonably homogenous, despite all these differences."[38]

In addition to this theological outline, the historical development of Sufi orders can be summarized in the following way: Although almost every single Sufi order relates itself to Prophet Muhammad, peace and blessings be upon him, the history of Sufism starts with Hasan al-Basri (d.728) and Rabi'a al-Adawiya (d.801).[39] Hasan al-Basri represents self-possession, sobriety, and self-control, whereas Rabia represents ecstasy, rapture, and intoxication. Bayazid al-Bistami (d.874) and Abu'l-Qasim al-Junayd (d.910) continued these two traditions. In the 10th and 11th centuries Sufi ideas were systematized. The works of Ibn Arabi and those of al-Qushayri represent the two ends of the spectrum: Ibn Arabi is highly sophisticated while al-Qushayri is very accessible and understandable. Muhammad al-Ghazali (d.1111) is considered to be the person who reconciled Sufi ideas and Orthodox Muslim thought, two dimensions of Islam, with his *Ihya al-Ulumu'd-Din* (Revival of Religious Sciences).[40]

The Brotherhoods with Which Yunus Emre can be Associated

The Bektashi Order

The Bektashi order, both in terms of current religious and social structures of Turkish society and in terms of the place it holds in Yunus Emre scholarship, is one of the most important organizations to be considered. A discussion of the Bektashi order offers insights into both the poetry and personality of Yunus Emre. Here there are two main arguments. One group of scholars, including Abdülbaki Gölpınarlı[41] and İlhan Başgöz,[42] assert that Yunus Emre was a Bektashi and find enough evidence in his poetry to support this view. The second group, including Faruk Kadri Timurtaş,[43] Ahmet Kabaklı,[44] and Sezai Karakoç,[45] asserts that Yunus Emre had no relationship with the Bektashi order at all. The second group also present evidence from Yunus Emre's poetry and stories about him that support their opinion.

Since there is not enough convincing evidence to decide definitively whether Yunus Emre was a Bektashi or not, Yunus Emre's status as a Bektashi or non-Bektashi can only be dependent on the definition of the term Bektashi. By defining the basics of the order, we can attain a more reliable basis from which to discuss this question. When the term Bektashi is defined based on the main sources that pertain to the order, namely, the *Vilayetname*[46] and *Makalat*, Yunus Emre can be called a Bektashi. In other words, the theological content of the poetry of Yunus Emre is compatible with that of the main reference works of the Bektashi order. However, it is very difficult to conceive of Yunus Emre as associated with the order when it is defined in the following way. Gölpınarlı, for instance, discusses the impact of Yunus Emre on Alevi[47] Bektashi literature, and explicitly suggests that the source of such literature was Yunus Emre's poetry. In his discussion, he outlines the basic features of Alevi Bektashi literature, and goes one step further by illustrating what he views to be the commonalities between the poetry of Yunus Emre and that of Alevi Bektashi poets. He states:

> Alevi Bektashi literature mentions the beliefs of this group: that the light in the candle of power, that a razor touched someone in the assembly of Forty and bled forty of them, that a single grape was crushed and drunk by forty people, forty of them became intoxicated and began dancing, that a lion stopped Prophet Muhammad during the nocturnal journey (*mi'raj*), that Muhammad followed the word of Gabriel and gave his ring to this lion and that the following morning Ali submitted the ring to Muhammad, the narratives of Hacı Bektaş Veli in the *Vilayetname*,...the traditions of Alevi-Bektashi saints.[48]

For Gölpınarlı other characteristics of this literature are:

> [. . .] *tawalla* and *tabarra*, [love for the family of the Prophet (*Ahl al-Bayt*) and enmity for the enemies of the family of the Prophet], Ali becoming God and Muhammad becoming secondary, a hatred for the Ottomans, love for the world and worldly things, criticism of Divine love, and critical attitudes towards formal aspects of religion, such as ablution or exaltation of the Ka'ba.[49]

After outlining these features, Gölpınarlı concludes by linking Yunus Emre to the order as he has defined it:

> [. . .] the light in the candle of power, Gabriel's being a teacher of Ali, the assembly of Forty, Uveys, the bleeding of forty with a razor, crushing a grape and its becoming a drink for forty people, four doors, forty states, love for the world, love for the beloved, criticism of the formal aspects of religion, moral thought... and a criticizing, mocking attitude. Yunus has all of these and Yunus is the first in all of these. Every Alevi and Bektashi certainly men-

> tions these. The only thing that Yunus does not have in his all-embracing thought is excessive hatred.[50]

Gölpınarlı makes a number of explicit statements and implications in these paragraphs which seriously contradict the teachings of both Yunus Emre and Hacı Bektaş Veli. Unfortunately, the statements made by Gölpınarlı are repeated in many scholarly and popular works.[51] Gölpınarlı states that Muhammad becomes secondary and Ali becomes God in Alevi Bektashi literature, as well as there being an excessive love for the world and criticism for the formal aspects of the religion. By stating that only hatred for certain groups is not present in the works of Yunus Emre, Gölpınarlı explicitly suggests that these features, along with many others he mentions, apply to Yunus Emre.

First of all, it must be said that it is categorically not true that all of the works of Bektashi literature follow the criteria that Gölpınarlı presents. The best examples that can be given to refute this blanket categorization are the works of Hacı Bektaş Veli and the works attributed to him, such as the *Makalat* and *Vilayetname*. In neither of these works do we come across the features that Gölpınarlı claims all Alevi Bektashi literature contains. Irene Melikoff, a distinguished scholar on the Bektashi order, expresses this by saying that "[in the main sources of the Bektashi order] we cannot find any of the excessive elements which are the features of Bektashi literature."[52] Unfortunately, the modern reception and presentation of these works has fostered this idea. A revealing example of this misrepresentation is the information provided in the original text of the *Vilayetname* about the lineage of Hacı Bektaş. In the original text of the *Vilayetname*, both the prose and poetry versions, the lineage of Hacı Bektaş is traced back to Prophet Muhammad, peace and blessings be upon him, and Hacı Bektaş is explicitly referred to as a *sayyid*, a descendant of the Prophet.[53] However, in the introduction of the text in the Gölpınarlı edition, most probably in an effort to prove his idea that Muhammad had become secondary, Gölpınarlı traces the lineage of Hacı Bektaş back to Ali, leaving it there.[54]

In the *Vilayetname* there are numerous references to God and the Prophet, making it impossible to carve out a theological scheme like the one to which Gölpınarlı refers. There are many similarities between the motifs and events related in the *Vilayetname* and other sources that are important in the history of Islam. For example, Can Baba of Karadeniz is a local version of the story of Abraham being thrown into the fire,[55] while Huy Ata's burning the idols[56] is again similar to Abraham's burning the idols and Sarı Saltuk's appearance in more than one coffin is similar to the similar appearance by Ali or Uways al-Qarani.[57]

In Yunus Emre's poems we see exactly the opposite of what Gölpınarlı has suggested. For instance, Ali is mentioned eight times in the *Divan*, but interestingly, every time Yunus Emre mentions Ali, he also mentions Prophet Muhammad and/or the other three caliphs in the same poem, if not in the same couplet.* The idea of Muhammad being secondary and Ali gaining superiority over the other caliphs has absolutely no basis in the works of Yunus Emre. The fact that Anna Masala thought Yunus Emre had composed the best poems for the Prophet shows how some people view the same poetry in drastically different ways from Gölpınarlı.[58]

---

* *Ebu Bekr u Ömer ol din ulusu*
Aliyy-i Murtaza, Osman benümdür

("Abu Bakr, Umar who are the greatest of that religion
And Ali al-Murtaza and Uthman are mine.")

(Yunus Emre, II, p. 48)

Ömer u Osman Ali Mustafa yarenleri
Bu dördünün ulusı Ebu Bekr-i Siddikdur

("Umar, Uthman and Ali are the friends of Mustafa
The greatest of these four is Abu Bakr as-Siddiq.")

(Yunus Emre, II, p. 100)

Tanrı Arslanı Ali sağında Muhammed'in
Hasan ile Hüseyin solunda Muhammed'in

("The lion of God, Ali, is on the right side of Muhammad
Hasan and Husayn are on the left side of Muhammad.")

(Yunus Emre, II, p. 155)

See also Yunus Emre, II, pp. 102, 146, 246, 273, 321, 343 and 349.

The second issue in Gölpınarlı's description which is not in keeping with the poetry of Yunus Emre is his alleged critical attitude towards the formal aspects of religion, such as praying and visiting the Ka'ba for pilgrimage. In many places Yunus Emre emphasizes the importance of formal religious practices. In fact, he goes one step further and suggests that people discover the meanings behind these formal aspects, thereby acquiring a deeper understanding of God, creation, and related religious issues. Tatçı suggests that Yunus Emre is the first person to have composed poems in a genre called *salatname*, which is mainly concerned with the importance of ritual prayers.[59] In fact, in at least seven poems Yunus Emre specifically addresses the issue of ritual prayers.[60]

In addition to these striking examples, there are other examples in Gölpınarlı which demonstrate that the asserted similarities between the poetry of Yunus Emre and Alevi Bektashi literature do not exist. These include Archangel Gabriel acting as the teacher of Ali, the world as the destination of love, and the beloved as a real person, not as God. In the poetry of Yunus Emre, Gabriel is always associated with Prophet Muhammad, not with Ali.* Yunus Emre criticizes love for this world in many poems. Only in a few poems out of the four hundred and sixteen that he wrote does Yunus Emre mention a real person as the beloved. This does not mean that a real person does not appear as the beloved in Sufi poetry; rather, this phenomenon simply does not exist in the work of Yunus Emre.

---

* *Muhammed'e bir gece Çalab'dan indi burak*
Cebrail eydir hacem Mirac'a kiğirdi Hak

("One night Burak came down for Muhammad
Gabriel told him that God calls for the Ascension.")
(Yunus Emre, II, p. 143)

Gitdi Cibril hazreti getirdi Burak atı
Nurdan idi hilati gözi gevher yüzi ak

("Gabriel went and brought the Burak horse
His cloth was from light, his eyes were gems and his face was pure white.")
(Yunus Emre, II, p. 143)

In the poem in question, Yunus Emre describes a beautiful woman, but finishes the poem by tying this love to Divine love: "Yunus saw the disclosure of God in you / There is no way that he can leave you since God has been seen in you."[61] Moreover, the claim that the destination of love is this world is simply baseless. The world and love for worldly objects are depicted in the poetry of Yunus Emre as grave dangers for Sufis. In many poems Yunus Emre warns against the transitory and deceptive nature of the world, emphasizing the importance of eternal life.*

This understanding of the poetry of Yunus Emre as exemplifying Alevi Bektashi beliefs is not peculiar to Gölpınarlı; his perspective is shared by many others and has become tied to the understandings of the Bektashi order in particular and religion in general during the modern period. There are two issues that need to be dealt with in regards to this matter; the first one is the historical development of the Bektashi order, while the second is the attitude of modern intellectuals towards the Bektashi order and other religious institutions.

It is known that the Bektashi order began in the thirteenth century under the guidance of Hacı Bektaş Veli; like many other brotherhoods, it was only formed as an order sometime later by his disciples. Balım Sultan (d.1519), who is also known as *pir-i sani*

---

* *Bu dünyanın meseli ulu bir şara benzer*
("This world is like a great city.")
(Yunus Emre, II, p. 86)

Gerekmez dünya bize çünkü baki bünyad değil
("We do not need the world since it is not permanent.")
(Yunus Emre, II, p. 163)

Mani eri bu yolda melul olası değil
("The man of meaning should not be downhearted on this path.")
(Yunus Emre, II, p. 167)

Zinhar virmegil gönül dünya payına birgün
("Never fall in love with the world.")
(Yunus Emre, II, p. 257)

(the second patron saint), is credited with the formal establishment of the order. Although there was tension between the Seljukid state and Bektashi circles at the beginning because of their connection to the *baba*s and the Baba İshak rebellion (1240), over time this tension disappeared and the Bektashis became supporters of the new authority, the Ottomans. In the *Vilayetname*, we can find support for Osman Gazi, the founder of the Ottoman dynasty.[62] From historical sources, we know that the Bektashi order can be considered, in a way, to have been a state-sponsored brotherhood and an important element in the Janissary corps. In fact, the Ottoman sultans had the tomb of Hacı Bektaş repaired twice.[63]

During the fifteenth century, however, mainly for political reasons, there was separation between the Bektashis who were living in the western and the eastern parts of the empire. The political reason behind this separation was Iranian propaganda directed towards the Bektashis in the eastern part of the empire. This propaganda was transmitted through various means, such as poetry,[64] theology, and politics.[65] Eventually the eastern Bektashis became politically anti-Ottoman. The Bektashis' attitude towards the Janissaries and the Janissaries' attitude towards them was a clear sign of this distinction. For example, the Janissaries were not willing to fight against western Bektashis, although they considered eastern Bektashis to be their enemies; eastern Bektashis viewed the Janissaries in the same way.[66] This political division brought theological differences too. Eastern Bektashis were very much influenced by Shiite doctrine. In some Turkish poems[67] that parallel those of Yunus Emre, Shah Ismail (d.1524), the founder of the Safavid dynasty in Iran, replaces the word "you", meaning God, in the original with Ali.[68] Although Shah Ismail lost the battle at Çaldıran in 1514, in a way he was able to win the battle in the political arena by gaining the sympathy of many Ottoman subjects, particularly in the eastern part of the country.

The separation between eastern and western Bektashis continued until 1826, a turning point for the western Bektashis. In this year, Mahmud II abolished the Janissaries, closed all the Bektashi *tekke*s (lodges), and executed many Bektashi sheikhs. The main reason for this was their close affiliation with the Janissary corps; there was no theological reason for Mahmud II's actions that caused them to be directed towards the Bektashis per se. After this event, eastern and western Bektashis shared a similar anti-Ottoman sentiment, although the reasons were completely different. This anti-Ottoman sentiment continues to be the case, even today. In the writings of many Turkish scholars and intellectuals who identify themselves as Alevi-Bektashi or who are sympathetic to this religious orientation it is rarely mentioned that the Bektashi order was on good terms with the Ottoman state until 1826. In these writings, the period after 1826 marks the beginning of Bektashi history.

The reason for this understanding is closely related to the attitude in modern Turkey towards Islam in general and the brotherhoods in particular. In the modern period, all the brotherhoods were banned as they were considered to be a barrier to the pursuit of a modern way of life. The Bektashi order, which had continued to exist as a minor brotherhood after 1826, suffered a blow from this strict policy. In a novel published in 1925 Yakup Kadri (1889–1974), one of the major ideologues of the Republican period, described a Bektashi sheikh as a womanizer.[69] For Schimmel and earlier for Birge, this sort of negative portrayal of Bektashis by Turkish intellectuals is what led to the banishment of the brotherhoods and is perceived as being in harmony with the teaching of Kemalism.[70]

In recent scholarship and the popular understanding of the Bektashi order two trends have overlapped: the anti-Ottoman sentiment that has continued since the 15th century among the eastern Bektashis and since 1826 among the western Bektashis, and the attitude of some other modern intellectuals against religion, which started with attempts at Westernization towards the end of the Ottoman period. In the first trend, the Bektashi order is portrayed as being in contradiction with the Ottoman state and its Sunnite theology. In the second trend, after disassociating the Bektashi order from the Ottoman state and Sunni Islam, the modern view of religion considers the Bektashi order, along with other religious institutions, to be a "childish and primitive way of thinking and reasoning, characteristic of primitive societies."[71] This is not confined to the Bektashi order; both Gölpınarlı and some other modern scholars feel similarly about the Malami order. After describing Malamatis as honest and sincere devotees of religious understanding in a highly positive language, Gölpınarlı and Murat Bardakçı state that the last Malamis passed away in the 1960s;[72] it is as if they were an endangered species of animal, not the followers of a religious understanding.

In conclusion, it would not be wrong to say that the teachings of Hacı Bektaş Veli and the philosophical content of the poetry of Yunus Emre are very similar and that there is a strong parallel between the two. However, when the Bektashi order is described in regional terms, as in the case of the eastern Bektashis, or historically, as in the case of the post-1826 period, it is very difficult to find a similarity between the poetry of Yunus Emre and the teachings of the Bektashi order. This aspect of the poetry of Yunus Emre forces us to reconsider the limited understanding of the Bektashi order and to evaluate it with its historical dimensions and the commonalities that it shares with other Sufi orders, without dismissing its distinctive features.

The Malami-Qalandari Order

As we will evaluate Yunus Emre in the context of the 13th and 14th century Muslim world, an overview of the major Sufi orders of his time would help us to better understand his ideas and poetry. Unfortunately, we do not have detailed historical and biographical information about the life of Yunus Emre or the specific brotherhood to which he might have belonged. There are only certain assumptions about which brotherhood he may have belonged to based on his spiritual teachers and his poetry. For instance, it is evident from his poetry that he was a disciple of Tapduk Emre and Barak Baba.* There is ample information about Barak Baba and the fact that he was a Malami Qalandari sheikh.[73] In this case, it seems reasonable to assume that Yunus Emre was a Malami Qalandari dervish, since he openly expresses in his poems that Tapduk Emre and Barak Baba were his sheikhs.[74]

However, there are legitimate questions about this assumption, just as there are legitimate questions as to what the real nature of the Malami order was. The word Malami comes from the Arabic root *lam-waw-mim*, commonly translated as "blame, reproach,"[75] and *malami* is often rendered as "people of blame." Some scholars, such as Gölpınarlı, assert that the Malami were a brotherhood which historically distinguished itself from the others, even working against other brotherhoods as a group with a secret belief system.[76] The second group of scholars, among them being Seyyed

---

* *Yunus'a Tapdug ve Saltug u Baraktandır nasip*
Nasip çün gönülden cuş kıldı ben nasıl pinhan olam

("Blessings for Yunus are from Taptuk, Saltug and Barak
My heart desires it heavily, how can I avoid it?")
(Yunus Emre, II, p. 217)

Vardığımız illere şol safa gönüllere
Baba Tapduk manisin saçtık elhamdulillah
Tapduğun tapusunda kul olduk kapısında
Yunus miskin çiğ idik piştik elhamdulillah

("To the lands we arrived, to the hearts that are happy
Thank God, we spread the message of Baba Tapduk
In the lodge of Tapduk we became servants
Yunus was raw, thank God we were cooked.")
(Yunus Emre, II, p. 297)

Yunus bir doğan idi kondi Tapduk koluna
Avın şikare geldi bu yuva kuşu değil

("Yunus was a falcon and perched on the hand of Tapduk
The bird came to the hunter; this is not a bird of the nest.")
(Yunus Emre Divanı, II, p. 172)

Hossein Nasr, suggests that *malami* is a type of umbrella concept that originated from Qur'anic verses and hadiths and was an important tradition in Sufi brotherhoods.[77]

For Ibn Arabi, for instance, *malami* is a concept that can be considered to be a stage at which some people are found or which people pass through to reach God or perfect themselves. It is considered to be the final stage on the way to perfection. The people who are at this stage reflect the Divine Names of God without a claim of Lordship or without giving credit to their egos; they become ordinary men. The fact that, at least in the Turkish case, people from various brotherhoods would call themselves *Malami* attests to the validity of this understanding.[78] In various Sufi brotherhoods we see that this is expressed in different ways. In the Naqshibandi, for example, it is formulated as renouncing the world (*tark ad-dunya*), renouncing the Hereafter (*tark al-uqba*), renouncing existence (*tark al-hasti*), and renouncing renunciation or complete surrender (*tark at-tark*). The word *Malami* basically refers to a Qur'anic verse that describes the virtue of a believer as someone who is not afraid of being blamed by others.[79]

One reason that some scholars consider Malamis and other Sufis to be separate categories is the famous passage from the *Meccan Openings* by Ibn Arabi. As Chittick puts it, Ibn Arabi uses "the term 'Sufi' not as a generic term for the seekers and finders of God, but as a designation for a particular type of spirituality which entails a certain amount of outward show and self-satisfaction, and thus denotes certain friends of God who are less than perfect."[80] Ibn Arabi refers to three groups of people: the first group is dominated by renunciation, the second group is Sufis, and the third is the people of blame, the Malamis. Ibn Arabi describes this group in the following way:

> The third group adds nothing to the five daily prayers or the supererogatory exercises (*rawatib*). They do not distinguish themselves from the faithful who perform God's obligations by any extra state whereby they might be known. They walk

> in the market, they speak to the people, and none of God's creatures sees any of them distinguishing themselves from the common people by a single thing; they add nothing to the obligatory works or the Sunna among the common folk. They are alone with God, firmly rooted, not wavering from their servanthood for the blink of an eye. They find no pleasure in leadership, since Lordship has overcome their hearts and they are lowly before it. God has given them knowledge of the places of things and of appropriate works and states. They are veiled from creatures and stay concealed from them by the covering of the common people. For they are sincere and purely devoted servants of their Master; they witness Him constantly in their eating and drinking, their waking and sleeping are with Him among the people... Both outwardly and inwardly they maintain for themselves the name by which God has named them, that is, the "poor."...The People of Blame do not distinguish themselves from any of God's creatures by anything, so they are unknown. Their state is the state of the common people.[81]

The main characteristic of Malami-Qalandaris is that they reject an understanding of Sufism based on praying to God with fear of punishment or hope of entering into Heaven. Malamis are considered to be from the school of Rabia, who was said to have rushed in the street with a jug of water in one hand and fire in the other. When she was asked what she was doing she said: "I am going to put out the fire of Hell with water and burn down Heaven with fire so that people will pray only for the love of God, not for the fear of Hell or the hope of Heaven." According to this understanding, human beings can reach true happiness or perfection by loving God truly and by blaming their carnal and worldly desires and ego (*nafs*). The reason that certain Malami-Qalandaris dressed in a ridiculous manner stems from this idea. Since they wanted to arrange their whole life according to what God wants, they desired to be criticized by people in order to be secure from the danger of being appreciated by them.

In various places in his *Divan* Yunus Emre uses the main motifs of the Malami-Qalandaris.

If I am really in love with you, I should not be afraid of reproach
I should be able to sacrifice my soul with pleasure; I should be able to dress in the garments of reproach.*

We did not reach here by hypocrisy
Let those who dressed in the garments of reproach be with us.**

Since Malami-Qalandaris reject an understanding of religion that is solely based on ritual prayers they are frequently criticized and accused of not being good believers. However, we should not forget that other people who were outcasts of society used a similar discourse to excuse their situation; although they had nothing to do with Sufis, they covered up their actions by pretending to be Malamis.

The second distinct feature of Malami-Qalandaris is that they traveled to observe the reflections of Divine love, to read the book of the universe in order to appreciate the creation, and to disseminate their ideas and experiences to other people. It is evident from Yunus Emre's poetry that he traveled to many places.***

The assumption that Yunus Emre was a Malami Qalandari dervish is based on the arguments outlined above. However, it is diffi-

---

* *Gerçek sana aşık isem arlanmaklık nemdür benim*
Şükrane canım virem melamet tonum giyem.
(Yunus Emre, II, p. 225)

** *Hele biz işbu yola gelmedik riyayile*
Bu melamilik tonun bizimle giyen gelsin.
(Yunus Emre, II, p. 249)

*** *Varduğumuz illere şol safa gönüllere*
Baba Tapduk manisin saçdık elhamdulillah.

("To the lands in which we arrived, to the hearts that are happy
Thank God, we have spread the message of Baba Tapduk.")
(Yunus Emre, II, p. 297)

Gezdüm Urumila Şam'ı yukaru illeri kamu
Çok istedim bulımadım şöyle garip bencileyin.

("I traveled in Anatolia and Damascus and all the upper lands
I searched hard but could find no poor one like me.")
(Yunus Emre, II, p. 284)

cult to say these features belong exclusively to Malami Qalandari dervishes. First of all, just because the sheikh of Yunus Emre was a Qalandari does not categorically mean that Yunus Emre was a Qalandari, too. At this time there were many Sufi teachers organizing, gathering, and training people from every walk of life with or without a formal sheikh-disciple relationship. If a master-disciple relation is to be accepted as a determining factor, then we would have to say that Tapduk Emre was a Bektashi because he was a student of Hacı Bektaş Veli, and similarly, Hacı Bektaş Veli was a Yesevi since he was a student of Ahmed Yesevi. This of course, is not reasonable, and thus it cannot be categorically stated that Yunus Emre was a Malami merely because he was affiliated with a Malami sheikh.

The second argument is that Malami Qalandari dervishes traveled a great deal and we can see that Yunus Emre also did this, thus possibly indicating that he was a Malami Qalandari dervish. However, in this period traveling was a very common practice for both social and religious reasons. There are many well-known Sufi names of the time, such as Rumi, Ibn Arabi, Bahauddin Walad, the father of Rumi, Fakhruddin Iraqi, and Najmuddin Kubra; all of these belonged to various brotherhoods and traveled more than Yunus appears to have done. Secondly, in many places the Qur'an advises believers to make journeys, both physically and metaphorically.[82] Indeed, the Muslim calendar starts with a journey, the emigration of Prophet Muhammad from Mecca to Medina in 622.

All in all, it is very difficult to depict Yunus Emre as a member of a Malami-Qalandari order of dervishes; these dervishes have much in common with other groups as well as displaying a great variety in terms of social class and the understanding and application of Sufi elements. On the one hand, we see some Qalandari dervishes dressing strangely (half-naked or covered with animal skins), while there are other Qalandari dervishes who criticize such behavior. It would be reasonable to suggest that Malami Qalandaris were a major Sufi group that gave birth to other brotherhoods in Anatolia. The use of the words Malami and Qalandari by the two great names of the time, Ibn Arabi and Rumi, reinforces this notion. Confining Yunus Emre and his poetry to a specific group deprives him of his place within the greater context of the Sufi world in the 13th and 14th centuries. It is very important that the poetry and ideas of Yunus Emre should be analyzed by relating them to the general worldview and Sufi understanding of the time, rather than by relating him to a very specific group, particularly since there is not a great deal of reliable information about the group or the relationship he may have had with the group.

Yunus Emre's Relationship with Rumi

Eric Auerbach (1892–1957), who is considered to be one of the founders of the study of comparative literature, describes his peculiar situation at the time of writing the book *Mimesis* in Istanbul in 1946. He states that he is writing a book which aims to show that European countries share a cultural continuum and that literature is a good realm to prove this continuity. It is ironic that he could not stay in Europe because he was Jewish and was able to find safety only in Istanbul.[83] This anecdote is more than just an interesting personal story. In a way, it summarizes at least one major aim of comparative studies and the implicit reasoning behind studying different authors, poets and texts across cultures. Auerbach aims to show the interconnectedness and closeness of the cultures of European countries based on literary works. The samples that he chooses naturally support his theory. The authors discussed in his book range from Homer to Virginia Woolf. His main thesis is the essential unity of European culture. He takes Europe as a whole, in and of itself, which reflects this unity. He also suggests that a work of literature cannot be properly appreciated or criticized independent of its cultural matrix.

When we study the works on Yunus Emre, what we observe is very similar to what Auerbach has tried to achieve. In this case, what is involved is a source culture, Turkish culture, and a target culture, that is, European culture. The names of poets whose works have been compared to those of Yunus Emre, such as Dante and Camus, and from a broader perspective, the names that are compared with Turkish authors in comparative literature, strongly suggest that there is or has to be an inherent similarity between European culture and Turkish culture. In this matter, the underlying assumption becomes prescriptive and literature, or literary studies, becomes an ideology, as Terry Eagleton has claimed.[84] At this juncture, the aim of literary studies has overlapped with the aim of political ideology in the last two centuries in Turkey, that is, to reach the level of modern, contemporary civilization (*muasır medeniyet* or *çağdaş uygarlık seviyesi*). One should keep in mind that in the Turkish case, "modern" or "contemporary" is interchangeable with "Western." Although there are few exceptions, the fact that Western names are overwhelmingly used in comparative literature in the Turkish case proves this statement in the area of literary studies. In a national comparative literature symposium held in 2001 in Turkey, out of 52 talks, only two focused on links between Turkish and non-European literatures.[85]

Comparing Yunus Emre with other poets, both European and non-European, from various centuries might have its own benefits. For instance, considering how literary works have been used to emphasize a golden past for nations in the age of nationalism, such as the case of fraudulent manuscripts that were supposed to prove a golden age of Czech poetry,[86] or the case of another forgery, James Machperson's *Fingal*[87] in 1762, it would be useful to demonstrate how Yunus Emre has been used to retrospectively construct a national literature and history.

However, in order to understand the cultural context and poetry of Yunus Emre, one has to compare him with those who shared the same cultural and historical world. In the 13th century there were three major sources for the enrichment of culture in Anatolia; these were Andalusia and North Africa, represented in particular by Ibn Arabi, the Middle East and Central Asia, which were, in the case of Yunus Emre, represented by Ahmed Yesevi, and Iran, represented by

Shams Tabrizi in the case of Rumi.[88] Therefore, by comparing at least some of the basic elements in the poetry of Yunus Emre with that of Rumi we can arrive at useful results.

Comparison of the poetry of Yunus Emre and that of Rumi in terms of the major themes in their poetry, which are the concepts of love, death, and providing advice, reveals the undeniable similarities and commonalities between them. One should take into consideration that Rumi composed his poetry in Persian because of his education, his location in the predominantly Persian-speaking center of the Seljukid state, and the cultural trends of his time, whereas Yunus Emre composed his poetry in Turkish mostly because of the intended function of his poetry, which was to educate the Turkish-speaking masses.

Yunus Emre makes explicit mention of Rumi, who died when Yunus Emre was about 35, and who lived in the same geography. Although there is no reliable information about whether they met, it is clear from the poetry of Yunus Emre that he was well aware of Rumi's presence and poetry.

> From the time Rumi Hudavendgar looked at us
> His majestic glance is the mirror of our heart.*
>
> In the conversation with Mevlana there was a wine party with saz;
> The Gnostic delved into the meaning since he is with angels.**
>
> Rumi said "Yunus! Stay in your place, speechless.
> Those who do not benefit from this conversation become aggressive."***

---

* *Rumi Hudavendgar bize nazar kılalı*
Anun görklü nazarı gönlümüz aynasıdır
(Yunus Emre, II, p. 64)

** *Mevlana sohbetinde saz ile işret oldu*
Arif maniye taldı çün biledir ferişte
(Yunus Emre, II, p. 301)

*** *Yunus eydür Rumi epsem otur yerinde*
Bu sohbete doymayan sonra savaşgan olur
(Yunus Emre, II, p. 58)

Fakih Ahmed Kutbuddin, Sultan Sayyid Najmuddin
Rumi Jalaluddin… Where are all these axes of the universe?*

The way both Sufi poets consider love is very similar. For both, love is the element that distinguishes human beings from other creatures in the world.

Every animal knows what love is, the wolf, rooster or lion.
He who is blind to love is lower than a dog.[89]

Do not give advice to those who do not have love;
A human being without love is like an animal; an animal cannot benefit from advice.**

Listen, O friends, love resembles the Sun;
The heart without love resembles a stone.***

Both poets also take love as the reason for the creation of existence, in keeping with a hadith qudsi, "I was a Hidden treasure and I wanted to be known and thus created the universe." Here, love is the reason for the creation of the world.

Before the earth and heavens existed, the building of love existed.
Love existed from the beginning; whatever exists was brought by love.****

Love is also considered to be the major cause of change in the world and it determines a Sufi's position towards other creatures.

---

* *Fakih Ahmed Kutbuddin Sultan Seyyid Necmuddin*
Rumi Celaleddin ol kutb-i cihan hani
(Yunus Emre, II, p. 58)

** *Isksuzlara verme öğüt öğüdünden alır değil*
Işksuz adem hayvan olur hayvan öğüt bilir değil
(Yunus Emre, II, p. 166)

*** *İşidin ey yarenler aşk bir güneşe benzer*
Aşkı olmayan gönül mesel-i taşa benzer
(Yunus Emre, II, p. 83)

**** *Evvel yir gök yoğidi varidi ışk bünyadı*
Işk ezelden kadimdir ışk getirdü ne varın
(Yunus Emre, II, p. 263)

Both poets, in strikingly similar ways, explain the power of love and how the love that they feel for God has compelled them to love all creatures merely because they have been created by God.

> Love makes the ocean boil like a kettle
> And makes the mountains like sand.[90]
>
> Bitterness becomes sweet from love.[91]
>
> It makes seas rage and boil,
> Throws huge waves into turmoil,
> And moves the rocks off the soil;
> Love is a vigorous thing.[92]

The number seventy-two is used both in the poetry of Rumi and Yunus Emre to refer to all of humanity. They both love seventy-two nations because of their love for the Creator.

> For the religion of love knows no difference between seventy-two sects: it is different from all religions.[93]
>
> Those who do not regard seventy-two nations as the same
> Even if they are a saint, are to be considered an outlaw in reality.*

In the works of both poets love has two major parts: First, the Sufi poet reaches God and then he enjoys the happiness of spiritual union. For this very reason, death is seen as a gate through which the Beloved is attained. The way both poets approach the idea of death, a major element in Sufi understanding, shows the inherent similarities between them, as well as helping to invalidate the idea that the Sufi understanding is different from the position prescribed by the Islamic faith. Rumi considers death to be a gate through which human beings reach a higher form of life, as long as they follow the guidelines:

> I died as mineral and became plant,
> I died as plant and rose to animal,[94]

---

* *Yetmiş iki millete bir göz ile bakmayan*
Şer'in evliyasıysa hakikatte asidir

(Yunus Emre, II, p. 138)

I died as animal and I was a man,
Why should I fear? When did I become less by dying?[95]

The second aspect of love is suffering, which is considered to be an important part of love in Sufi poetry, as well as in Ottoman poetry in general.[96] In one way, persevering through the pain and misery of being separated from the Beloved demonstrates that the lover feels genuine love. Both Rumi and Yunus Emre ask God, the Beloved, not for the rewards that He gives, such as His mercy or salvation, but for Himself.

What does the ascetic seek? Your mercy (*rahmat*).
What does the lover seek? Your pain (*zahmat*).[97]

If that Friend kills me seventy times like Jirjis,
Even if He says I should die one thousand times more, I would come forward again.*

It is happiness for a person if he burns in the fire of love.
If the smoke emerges, the house becomes light.

I am happy with that fire, even if I burn a thousand times a day.
See how the moth sacrifices its soul in front of the candle.**

What they call Heaven is a few houses and a few *houris*.
Give them to those who ask for them, what I need is You, You.

What you call Heaven or My Heaven, and encourage the believers in
Is nothing but a house and a few *houris*, which I have no desire to embrace.

---

* *Cercisleyin ol dost beni yetmiş kez öldürür ise*
Bin kez dahi ölsün dese yüz bin kez ilerü gelem
(Yunus Emre, II, p. 190)

** *Devlet durur ol kişiye yanarısa aşk oduna*
Acı tütüni çıkıcak aydın olısar bu hane

Razıyam ol oda ben günde bin kez yanarısam
Gör nice can fida kılır şemi öninde pervane
(Yunus Emre, II, p. 299)

Give them to austere people; what I need is You, You.
How can I leave You for a house and a trellis?*

The place of ritual prayers is very important in connection with the place of love in the works of the two Sufi poets. It is very common that due to the intensity and twofold nature of meaning in Sufi poetry that both poets could be described as people who do not practice Muslim ritual prayers. However, both consider ritual prayers as intimate conversations with God and are very careful about following the guidelines to become a good Muslim. Yunus Emre repeatedly mentions the importance of the five daily prayers, fasting, giving alms, and pilgrimage. The fact that he emphasizes the importance of the human heart by saying:

An elderly man with a white beard,
Cannot know what his situation is.
He should not waste his time for pilgrimage
If he has broken a heart.**

should not overshadow his strict adherence to religious rituals. In at least seven poems Yunus Emre specifically emphasizes the importance of ritual prayers and shows he considers praying to be a requirement of being a Muslim.[98] Both Rumi and Yunus Emre can be regarded as people whose mystical experience is deepened by ritual prayers. The biography of Rumi also supports this idea. In one of the most important sources about his life and the best biographical source on Rumi, *Manaqib al-Arifin*, the author mentions that in addition to the five daily prayers Rumi would perform super-

---

* *Uçmak uçmağim dediğin müminleri yeltediğin*
Bir ev ile birkaç huri hevesim yok kuçmak için

Sofilara ver sen anı bana seni gerek seni
Ben nice terkedem seni bir evu çardağiçün

(Yunus Emre, II, p. 247)

** *Ak sakallu pir koca bilmezki hali nice*
Emek yimesin Hacca bir gönül yıkarısa

(Yunus Emre, II, p. 305)

erogatory nightly prayers (*tahajjud*), he would retire into seclusion during the month of Ramadan (*inziwa*) and practice ascetic austerities (*riyada*).[99]

> Hunger is the food of God with which He quickens the bodies of the very faithful.
> Hunger is a treasure which is preserved with God, who gives it to His special friends.[100]

Rumi uses different images, such as stairs, a ladder, and a minaret, to express the importance of the ritual prayers; he considers strict adherence to the rituals as prescribed in the Qur'an to be the first step on the ladder or the first brick in the minaret.

> This prayer and fasting, pilgrimage and striving on the way of God give witness to the faith.
> These alms and gifts and abandonment of envy
> give witness to your own secret.[101]

He even talks about all the different rituals and their importance in becoming a true Sufi.

> Although faith is built upon five pillars,
> Yet, by God, the greatest pillar of these is fasting.
> But He has hidden in all five the value of fasting,
> Just as the blessed Night of Power is hidden in fasting.[102]

Yunus Emre also emphasizes the importance of ritual prayers:

> The person who calls himself a Muslim should know the requirements of it.
> He should follow the order of God and pray five times daily.*

Both poets are very careful not to make the fulfillment of religious obligations a means of creating a privileged position among in-

---

* *Müslümanım diyen kişi şartı nedir bilse gerek*
Tanrının buyruğun tutup beş vakt namaz kılsa gerek
(Yunus Emre, II, p. 146)

dividuals. Rituals should stay between God and the individual, and only God, not the people, can decide who the better individual is:

> The one who says, "I do not pray," "I do"...
> Whether I do or not, only God knows my prayers.
>
> Nobody knows who is Muslim and who is not other than God.
> I perform my prayers if God accepts.*

Both Sufi poets, however, suggest going beyond a formal, artificial understanding of these prayers and delving into them to grasp their inner meaning. The ritual prayers are only signs of and tools to reach God. A true believer should search for the meaning behind the prayers, which will enable them to get closer, or gain proximity, to God.

> Our God says prostrate and draw near.[103]
> The prostration of our bodies becomes the proximity of the Soul.[104]
>
> If you break a heart, even once, the prayer you perform is no good at all.
> Nobody from the seventy-two nations will love or respect you.**
>
> The heart is the throne of God; God cares about the heart.
> Whoever breaks a heart is the unfortunate one of the two worlds.***

In addition to being tantamount to a clear reflection of an outpouring of love, one of the most significant aspects of the poetry of Rumi and Yunus Emre is the didactic content of their works. Both

---

* *Bana namaz kılmaz diyen ben kılurum namazımı*
Kılurısam kılmazısam ol Hak bilür niyazımı
Hakdan artık kimse bilmez kafir müselman kim durur
Ben kıluram namazımı Hak geçirise nazımı
(Yunus Emre, II, p. 349)

** *Bir kez gönül yıkdınısa bu kıldığın namaz değil*
Yetmiş iki millet dahi elin yüzün yumaz değil
(Yunus Emre, II, p. 166)

*** *Gönül Çalab'ın tahtı Çalap gönüle baktı*
İki cihan bedbahtı kim gönül yıkarise
(Yunus Emre, II, p. 306)

poets composed poetry to disseminate theories and ideas, rather than for artistic purposes. The specific expression used by Rumi to explain why he composed poetry and the style of his poetry, as well as his method of telling stories or parts of stories and drawing spiritual or moral lessons from them are all important indications that Rumi composed poetry in order to give advice.[105] One modern scholar is quite right in calling Rumi's poetry "another way to preach and pray"[106] and suggesting that "[with poetry] he got a better response among the general populace than more sedate and traditional forms of preaching."[107]

Yunus Emre also emphasizes the importance of giving advice, both by composing a sizeable amount of his poetry in a didactic style, including his long *mathnawi*, called *Risalatu'n Nushiyya (The Book of Advice)* and by specifically stating that he composed poetry to give advice. In many places Yunus Emre states that he composes poetry to reach people and to cleanse the dust from their hearts, an expression also used by Rumi.

> Yunus makes up these words as if adding honey to butter.
> He sells his property to the people; his load is gems, not salt.*
>
> In order to cleanse and rid the hearts of dust
> Speak that word which is the essence of the words.**

It is also very significant that both poets emphasize the Divine origin of their poetry and deny their own individuality in the process. In a way, they assert that what they are trying to achieve through their poetry is what God does with His Divine words. From this perspective, there is a commonality between the style used in the Qur'an and the style used in the *Mathnawi*. This, in par-

---

* *Yunus bu sözleri çatar sanki balı yağa katar*
Halka metaların satar yükü güherdir tuz degil
(Yunus Emre, II, p. 166)

** *Şu gönüller pasını yuyuban gidermeye*
Şol sözi söylegil kim sözün hülasasıdır
(Yunus Emre, II, p. 45)

ticular, applies to the matter of not telling the whole story, but giving just bits and pieces to make the point:

> Where am I and where is poetry? But into me breathes
> That one Turk who comes and says to me: Hey, who are you?[108]
>
> O, the one who knows the origins of words, come and tell where does this word come from?
> The one who does not know the origin of the words thinks that this word comes from me.*
>
> The word is not from black or white, it is not from reading or writing.
> It is not from this walking people, it comes from the voice of the Creator.**

In addition to the teaching purposes of the work of both poets, one should not forget the strong urge that is a result of mystic love. Both poets also express that they were compelled to write poetry when overwhelmed by the beauty and greatness of Divine Majesty. They wanted to share their experience with every one.

> "It was a great urge that compelled me to compose."[109]

This feeling is expressed by Yunus Emre even more strongly:

> "If I do not say that I love, the pain of love strangles me."***

---

* *Ey sözlerin aslın bilen gel di bu söz nerden gelir*
Söz aslını anlamayan sanır bu söz benden gelir
(Yunus Emre, II, p. 57)

** *Söz karadan aktan değil yazıp okumaktan değil*
Bu yürüyen halktan değül, Halik avazından gelir
(Yunus Emre,II, p. 58)

*** *Sevdüğüm söylemez isem sevmek derdi beni boğar*
(Yunus Emre, II, p. 94)

Chapter 2

An Analysis of Yunus Emre's Poetry

AN ANALYSIS OF YUNUS EMRE'S POETRY

The Didactic Function of Sufi Poetry in the 13th and 14th Centuries

Sufi circles use poetry for a variety of didactic purposes. The application of Sufi poetry in didactic contexts ranges from the training of disciples to the inducement of altered states of consciousness in ceremonies or rituals. The brotherhoods to which Yunus Emre may have belonged and for which he may have composed poems also used poetry in these manners. Although many scholars acknowledge that Sufi poetry served important didactic functions in the training and conduct of Sufi brotherhoods, this fact has often been neglected in interpreting the poetry of Yunus Emre. An examination of Yunus Emre's poetry for its didactic intent helps in the assessment of the overall meaning of his work. Furthermore, consideration of Yunus Emre's didactic aims helps us to understand and interpret poems that might otherwise seem obscure or elusive.

Historical evidence about Sufism in general and the history of the Bektashis, Mevlevis, and Qalandaris in particular indicate that poetry was used extensively in Sufi gatherings during the 13th and 14th centuries. It would be no exaggeration to say that poetry was important for the realm of Sufi ideation and imagination. Many poems that convey Sufi ideas also contain programmatic outlines for those who wished to attain enlightenment, such as disciples.[1]

In the case of Yunus Emre, the didactical aspects of his poetry are important. One legend mentions that Yunus Emre joined other disciples in gathering around a spiritual teacher; the latter requested that his students recite poetry. One day, the spiritual teacher asked one of his students, Yunus-i Güyende, to recite. However, Yunus-i Güyende was not able to recite any poems. The teacher then turned to Yunus Emre and asked him to recite. When Yunus Emre fulfilled this request, he realized that the time had come to compose poetry himself. This legend shows that the Sufi order that Yunus Emre aspired to join based its instructional methods in part on the recitation and production of mystical poetry.

Fuat Köprülü, who is the most significant scholar on Yunus Emre, discusses the issue of the educational aspect of the poetry of Yunus Emre and considers his poetry to be an inherent part of his teachings. In Köprülü's view, Yunus Emre is "a divine singer who calls out to explain to the heedless people the great truth that he has reached in his own words; a master poet who explains the disclosures of God."[2] Köprülü argues that Yunus Emre had a clear purpose for composing his poems and that he certainly was a moralist, trying to teach the values in which he believed.[3] There is certainly much textual evidence in the poetry of Yunus Emre that supports this statement.[4] However, in 1933, fifteen years after Köprülü's work, Burhan Toprak implicitly criticizes this view and asserts that Yunus Emre was not concerned with enlightening others; he was occupied with his own problems.[5] Starting from Toprak, the pedagogical aspect of the poetry of Yunus Emre has become lost at the expense of highlighting his artistic aspects, despite the fact that the educational and the artistic side are not mutually exclusive.

Yunus Emre expresses the idea that one of the main functions of his poetry is teaching or giving advice. In one of his particularly beautiful lines he says, "If I do not say that I love, the grief of love strangles me."[6] This refers to the basic Sufi idea that one has to be aware of and love God, and call on other people to experience the same thing. He also states that the words, the poetry, should be recited "to clean the dust" from the heart, which is more valuable than the Ka'ba, the most exalted place in Islamic belief.[7] The biographical evidence that we gather from Yunus Emre's poetry also supports this idea: He was a disciple of Tapduk Emre and went to many other places to spread the teaching of his mentor;* for Ahmet Yaşar Ocak this provides grounds for claiming that Yunus Emre was a Qalandari.[8]

There are many poems which can be explained more easily and which make better sense if we keep in mind the idea that Yunus Emre composed his poetry for liturgical and didactic purposes. The following poem, in which Yunus appears to be teasing God, a stance which is an exception when one considers the totality of his poems, provides a good example.[9]

O God if You would ever question me,
This would be my outright answer to Thee.

True, I have sinned, brutalizing my own being,
But what have I done against You, my King?

Did I make myself or I am Your creation?
Why drench me in sin, Benevolent One?

I saw dungeons when I opened my eyes,
Teeming with devils, temptation, and lies.

To shun death by hunger, many a time
In prison I had to eat dirt and grime.

Did Your dominion become any less?
Did I usurp any of Your prowess?

Are You hungry? Did I eat Your ration?
Did I deprive You, causing Your starvation?

You built me a bridge to cross, thin as hair.
Out of Your traps, I am to choose my own snare

---

* To the lands that we went, to the happy hearts
We spread the teaching of Baba Tapduk, thank God!
(Yunus Emre, II, p. 403)

If you want to clean the dust of the hearts
Speak that word which is the essence of the word.
(Yunus Emre, II, p. 45)

How can a man pass over a hair-thin bridge?
He falls, or clings on, or flies off the ridge?

Your slaves built bridges for the public good.
Those who pass over them head for the Godhead.

I hope that its firm foundation will not sway,
So that those who cross it will know this is the true way.

You set a scale to weigh deeds, for Your aim
Is to hurl me into Hell's crackling flame.

A scale is suitable for a grocer,
For a small merchant, or a jeweler

Sin, though, is the vilest, filthiest vice;
The profit of those unworthy of grace.

You can see everything, You know me fine;
Then why must You weigh all these deeds of mine?

Do You still seek revenge although You've killed me?
As I've rotted since darkest soil has filled me.

No harm ever came from Yunus to You;
Open, secret—all things are in your view.

God Almighty, why all this talk, why must
We prattle about a handful of dust?[10]

This poem can be, and has been, interpreted in several ways:[11] One interpretation is that Yunus Emre is making fun of the dogma, the basic principles, of religion. However, this interpretation poses problems when considered in relationship with the majority of his poems. If this exceptional poem is taken at face value, it poses a contradiction to the majority of Yunus Emre's work. In this case, two different Yunus Emres appear in the poetry. The first one is very enthusiastic about following the orders of God, and is not even content with this stage, but wants to ascend further. The second Yunus Emre criticizes the actions and attributes of God, rebelling against Him. This either has to be explained as a contradiction or inconsistency with the totality of his work, or there has to be another explanation. The pedagogical aspect of Sufi poetry solves the problem.

In the poem provided above, Yunus Emre expresses some of the ideas that all human beings struggle with in a simple, but effective way. On the personal level, one might ask the questions that Yunus asks when engaged in a dialogue with God or, indeed, in any endeavor along this path: One may argue, if God did not want human beings to commit sin then He would not have created sin or evil. Since God created evil, human beings should be forgiven for committing sins. If God knows and sees everything, as He is All-Knowing and All-Seeing, then why does He need angels and why does He oblige human beings to go through the process of "auditing", putting their sins and good deeds on scale like a grocer?

The poem is significant in terms of questioning the reasons behind the acts of God in relation to human beings and the degree and nature of their importance in creation. Although Yunus Emre calls the human being "a handful of dust," this is an ironic expression. It appears that he is criticizing the idea that the human being is not very important. Yunus has many other poems which indicate the central significance of human beings in the universe; indeed, based on this prevalent feature of his poetry some interpreters have called him a humanist.

The poetry, at least the genre in which Yunus Emre composed most of his poems—the *ilahi* (devotional hymn)—does not allow for the creation of separate voices in a single poem. That is to say, it is difficult to distinguish the voice of the poet. The *mathnawi* as a genre, on the other hand, provides an opportunity for the poet to express separate voices within the single unit, as in Yunus Emre's *Risalatu'n Nushiyya*. Thus, it would not be reasonable to take every single element, particularly in hymns, as the source of information from which one can draw conclusions about the personal feelings or ideas of the poet.

Rather than taking an apparent chastisement of God's acts at face value, Yunus Emre provides an opportunity to discuss the issues raised by the poem. It would not be a stretch of the imagination to state that Yunus Emre, and perhaps his spiritual teacher, discussed the attributes of God or the issue of predestination and free-will after this poem had been recited.

Most of the issues raised in this poem are problems not only in Islam, but also in other religions and teachings; they deal with the idea of God, creation, accountability and the Hereafter. Most of these questions, although expressed with a light attitude, are very serious. Discussions on these matters started from the first century of Islam and schools of thought have been established based on the differences in how one approaches these questions. For instance, the idea that God determines what one is going to do in life, and therefore how people can be held accountable for the things that they have to do is the basic premise of the Jabriya (pre-determinist).

They deny the freedom of the will and claim that the actions of the human being are subordinate to the compulsion (*jabr*) of God. In opposition to this, another school of thought, that of the Qadariya, asserts that "the actions of the human being are determined by the person themselves, not by God, and that the human being therefore possesses not only the power to act (*qudrat*) but also the power to determine their action and decree its effect,"[12] thus suggesting that the fact that a human is responsible for their actions and destiny has no affect on the actions of the human being at all. Both schools of thought have extreme and moderate representatives and have occurred in various forms in various geographies and times, with various consequences. For instance, the issue of whether God creates evil or creates evil acts is a topic of great debate. The famous Sufi Hasan al-Basri (642–728) argues that "God creates only good; evil stems from men or from Satan. Man chooses freely between the two; but God knows from all eternity what men will choose."[13] Another argument about whether God determines the actions of the human being is offered by Umar II, the Umayyid Caliph, (717–720), who argues that "God knows that one will sin, but also one could abstain from sin; His knowledge has only the function of recording, not of affecting (*hafiz*, not *nafidh*)."[14]

If one takes Sufism as a complete system that deals with every spiritual and social aspect of human beings, it becomes obvious that Sufism also deals with the questions and doubts that human beings might have. Sufism became such a widespread phenomenon because it was able to answer and solve the dilemmas and questions of human beings. In particular, the educational aspect of Sufi poetry fulfills this function. In many poems, Yunus Emre calls people to the destination that he has reached. One can even argue that the whole idea of his poetry fits the description of a road map. Two of the most common terms among Sufi orders are *sayr u suluk* (journeying and initiation) and the *salik* (initiate), or the traveler who follows a way to a goal and makes efforts to meet with God. Yunus Emre's *Risalatu'n Nushiyya,*[15] most likely composed in the second half of his life, has been largely ignored and labeled as a dry and didactic *mathnawi*. It is, however, a good example that demonstrates the educational aspect of the poetry of Yunus Emre. In this lengthy poem Yunus describes the impediments on the road, the beautiful things that are waiting at the end of the road, as well as the skills and requirements needed to reach to that end. Although this feature, that is the pedagogical elements, are found in many other poems, the *Risalatu'n Nushiyya* is the best example in terms of reflecting didactic quality both in its content and its tone. In this poem, Yunus, following the common tradition of Sufis of explaining religious concepts by using metaphors, figurative speech, and sometimes, farcical elements, presents the road map for the disciple on the path.

Risalatu'n Nushiyya is a book of advice and can easily be categorized as the textbook of a Sufi school. One can certainly see in its tone a similarity to a schoolteacher who is trying to make the topic of the course more comprehensible and interesting for the pupils. In this poem Yunus Emre discusses the creation of Adam, the four elements (fire, water, soil, and wind) of which the human being is believed to be composed, as well as the nature of the human being; among this latter he examines reason, belief, knowledge, the relations between spirit and reason, pride and contentment, anger, patience, stinginess and envy, gossip and calumny in a lively way by using the figures of the journey, the caravan, bandits, rivers, and oceans.

In this land of human attributes one can observe the struggle of the human being within themselves. The elements are presented in a way that in the end a human being will be wary of the pitfalls and perils of the Sufi road and be able to reach the ultimate point.

By using the human attributes as actual heroes, Yunus depicts a lively picture of struggle among various human faculties and demonstrates the troubles that a wayfarer might face. After the king Reason captured the land of Stinginess, Contentment became the new king. However there is a rebel in this land named Pride, who lives at the top of the mountains. Reason sends Modesty to take care of Pride; Modesty lets Pride run to the sea. Those who dive into this sea, which is the symbol for Divine unity or becoming part of the community rather than being alone, find pearls and corals. After Pride was overcome by what he found in the sea, other problems occur in the land, such as Order and Ease, which are the equivalents of extreme relaxation and extreme optimism. Reason sends Patience to take care of these. However, new problems such as Envy, Hatred, and Gossip cause some upheavals and discomfort. Reason pits Honesty against these and takes over control again. After this, the Thief, which is the symbol for Satan or the *nafs*, cannot find any place to live and leaves the land. Thus, the human being is able to complete their journey in the world by overcoming bodily desires and become a perfected human being.

Thematic Classification of the Poetry of Yunus Emre

A thematic classification of the poems of Yunus Emre gives a clear idea of the concerns and nature of his Sufi thought. It is possible to argue that one can determine the Sufi approach of the poet according to the number of poems he devoted to each theme. It is important to note that most of the poems in Yunus Emre's *Divan* can be categorized as *yekahenk*,[16] that is, a poem that can be specifically related to a single theme rather than more than one theme.

Yunus Emre wrote approximately 416 poems, including his long didactic poem called *Risalatu'n Nushiyya*.[17] The themes in the poetry of Yunus Emre can be listed, starting with those that have the greatest number, as poems about love, poems about death and the transitory nature of the world, poems about unity of being and the perfected human being, poems of a didactic nature, poems about the Prophet, poems about daily prayers, poems about social criticism, poems about nature, and poems about figurative love.

The love poems of Yunus Emre are specifically about Divine love, with only one exception. In one poem, Yunus Emre describes the beauty of a woman and at the end of the poem he says, "Yunus saw the appearance of God in your face, He cannot leave you because God has appeared in you,"* thus implying the Sufi idea of the manifestation of God (*tajalli*) in human beings. Although it is not uncommon in Sufi poetry to compose what are called figurative love poems, and although some parts of the poems of Yunus Emre can be read in this way, his love poems are overwhelmingly about Divine love.

Since love poems constitute the greatest number of poems in this *Divan*, symbolically the heart is of extreme importance. Sufis contend that the mind's capacity to reason and exercise free will links human beings to God, but the heart is the dwelling place of the soul. The mind, Yunus Emre maintains, has its purposes, but also its limits. Despite all the evidence of God that exists in others and the natural world, the mind alone cannot fathom the knowledge of God. The heart, on the other hand, intuits the inherent truth of God: "My heart does not obey the one who says the human form is clay/ I caused the essence of this clay to attain God, the

---

* *Yunus Hak tecellisin senin yüzünde gördü*
Çare yok ayrılmağa çün sende göründü Hak.
(Yunus Emre, II, p. 142)

Friend."* To Sufis, one who depends solely on intelligence and reason to judge the world sees the "form," but not the "essence" that is beyond the form. (In some Sufi texts, to be called intelligent or reasonable is more a form of criticism than a compliment.) As shown by the couplet above, Yunus Emre's poetry speaks of the relative importance of the heart. In other verses, he asserts that to break someone's heart is to nullify all the good deeds that have been performed over a lifetime. The overriding goal of the human soul is to love and praise God in appreciation of creation and in hope of reunion. Love, the Sufis teach, has a transformational power that affects all human faculties and which can bring one's heart closer to God. In the following verses, the speaker is an impassioned lover who expresses devotion to his beloved—God. As the beloved, God has the power to negate the egoistical self: "It is Your love that has taken me from me/ What I need is You, You/ I have been burning day and night/ What I need is You, You."**

Fixing on God as the beloved helps Yunus Emre—and other Sufis—to negate the ephemeral distractions of a passing world and to submerge himself into a higher consciousness. In the following couplet he expresses his pleasure at being freed from materiality by love: "Neither do I become happy for wealth / Nor do I become sorry for poverty / I am consoled with Your love/ What I need is You, You."*** God reciprocates. In this sense, the lover becomes the beloved of God, who uses omnipotence to free the individual from worldly concerns:

---

* *Suret topraktır diyeni gönlüm kabul etmez anı*
Bu toprağın cevherini hazrete irgürdüm ahi
(Yunus Emre, II, p. 373)

** *Aşkın aldı benden beni bana seni gerek seni*
Ben yanarım dünü günü bana seni gerek seni
(Yunus Emre, II, p. 383)

*** *Ne varlığa sevinürem ne yokluğa yerinürem*
Işkunila avunuram bana seni gerek seni
(Yunus Emre, II, p. 383)

"Your love kills lovers/ It makes the lovers dive into the ocean of love/ It fills them with manifestations/ What I need is You, You."*

For the Sufi who has attained a high level of awareness of God, life becomes an interminable waiting period. Detaching from the world, a perfected Sufi "dies before dying" and awaits the afterlife and the true destination of the soul—reunion with God.

The second greatest number of poems are concerned with death and the transitory nature of the world. The inevitability of death is a major theme in Yunus Emre's poems. To stress the ephemeral nature of life, these poems portray death grotesquely, warning people not to form false attachments.

> [Death] takes away the young and old, burns the mother's heart.
> It untangles the hair of blonde girls on the benches where corpses are washed.
>
> It takes away young lads in their prime and makes their mothers crazy
> It mixes the henna of brides with dirt.**

As in other poems, this one portrays the steps in the process of death in great detail. First, the angel of death takes the life out of the body. Then the corpse is carried to the graveyard. The verse goes on to describe the deceased's separation from loved ones and the burial. Finally, angels interrogate the deceased in the grave. The scene closes with the living quickly forgetting about the dead.***

---

* *Işkun aşıklar öldürür aşk denizine daldırır*
Tecelliyle toldurur bana seni gerek seni
(Yunus Emre, II, p. 384)

** *Alur yiğidi kocayı yakar ananın içini*
Kızların sarı saçını teneşirde çözer ölüm
Alur yiğidin âlâsın, divane eder anasın
Gelinlerin el kınasın topraklara karar ölüm.
(Yunus Emre, II, p. 211)

*** *Üç güne dek oturalar hep işini bitireler*
Ol dem dile getireler ayruk kimse anmaz ola
(Yunus Emre, II, p. 24)

In this macabre manner, the poems remind readers that they too must leave this world and that life is but a brief sojourn. Even beautiful things will pass. Couplets such as the following attest to the sensual attractiveness of the world: "This world is a bride dressed in green and red/ One cannot grow tired of looking at a new bride."* Other couplets warn the reader not to be taken in by the world's outward beauty: "Worshipping the world is like savoring a poisonous meal/ the one who cares about the end of life abandons the meal."** The aim is to redirect the reader's focus from worldly things to the transitory nature of life.

Devotion to God becomes an alternative to fears of mortality: "The world is the enemy of people; the goal is the Soul (God) of souls/ One should know that the world passes; abandon the world, my dear."*** Contrasting earthly time to cosmic time, the poems advise readers to prepare for inevitable death. In one of the most masterful and harmonious couplets of Turkish literature, Yunus Emre holds out the eternal reward of salvation for the faithful: "Why are you afraid of death?/ Don't be afraid! You will live forever."**** As a Sufi, Yunus Emre believed that all life is dedicated to God and all souls must return to God; this brings about a type of immortality that renders human mortality inconsequential.

The poet adopts two extreme positions against death. The first position is that he gruesomely describes the concept of death as a

---

* *Bu dünya bir gelindir yeşil kızıl donanmış*
Kişi yeni geline bakubanı toyamaz

(Yunus Emre, II, p. 116)

** *Dünyanın mahabbeti ağulu aşa benzer*
Ahirin sanan kişi ağulu aştan geçer

(Yunus Emre, II, p. 88)

*** *Dünya halkun düşmanıdır maksud ol canlar canıdır*
Bilinki dünya fanidir dünyayı terk etsen gönül

(Yunus Emre, II, p. 170)

**** *Ölümden ne korkarsın korkma ebedi varsın*

(Yunus Emre, II, p. 49)

terrifying experience. It would not be an exaggeration to call Yunus Emre the poet who composed the most terrifying death scenes in the realm of Turkish poetry.

The second position is exactly the opposite of the first attitude towards the concept of death. Here, Yunus Emre considers death to be a positive element, a gateway to eternity, to the Beloved for whom he has long yearned.

> Leave the worry of dying, the lover does not die, he is eternal.
> Dying has nothing to do with you because your soul is Divine.
>
> Why are you afraid of death? Don't be afraid, you will exist forever.
> If you make use of this, your argument has no meaning.
>
> Yunus, good news is for you, they call you toward God.
> The real word is "Everything is going to go back to its origin."*

For Yunus Emre, the human being is a guest; we are travelers in this world and are destined to return to our home, the home of the Friend, God:

> The person who comes to this world needs to leave eventually.
> He is a guest; he needs to travel to his hometown one day.
>
> We made a promise with that Friend before coming to this world.
> How much longer can we stay? The time is about to come.**

---

* *Ko ölmek endişesin aşık ölmez bakidir*
Ölmek senin ne ola çün canın ilahıdır

Ölümden ne korkarsın korkma ebedi varsın
Çünkim işe yararsın bu söz fasid davıdır

Yunus beşaret sana gel dirler dosttan yana
Külli şeyin ila aslih söz aslıdır

(Yunus Emre, II, pp. 49-50)

** *Bu dünyaya gelen kişi ahir yine gitse gerek*
Musafirdir vatanına birgün sefer etse gerek

Vade kıldık ol dost ile biz bu cihana gelmeden
Pes ne kadar eğlenevüz ol vademiz yitse gerek

(Yunus Emre, II, p. 149)

The poems about *insan al-kamil* (the perfected human being) and *wahdat al-wujud* (oneness of being, unity of being) also constitute a major theme in the poetry of Yunus Emre. According to the idea of oneness of being, the entire universe and everything in it is a manifestation of a single Being, that is, God. The creatures in the universe are signs (*ayat*) of this Being in various forms and contents. In no way should this be considered pantheism, since everything in the universe indicates or signifies God, while nothing but God can be god. If one can reach the level of the perfected human being, one can experience the unity of being and see the universe from this perspective.

> I am the eternal, I am the everlasting, I am the One who is the Soul for the souls.
> I am the One who helps those who have come off the road and become immured.
>
> I made these lands a plain; I put these mountains as a weight.
> I made the heavens a roof; I am the One who holds them up.
>
> I am the One who makes it snow, I am the One who freezes; I am the One who gives sustenance to animals.
> Know this, I am the One who is All-Compassionate and All-Merciful to the creatures.*

Yunus Emre also states that his unusual power, his so-called Godlike features, comes from his attachment, his allegiance to God; it is through this that he completely rids himself of his own ego. He states that he is more powerful since he has joined the Ocean of Divine Majesty. For this reason, his Godlike attitude is a confirmation of his acceptance of God, not a sign of rebellion against God.

---

* *Evvel benem ahir benem canlara can olan benem*
Azup yolda kalanlara hazır medet eden benem

Düz döşedim bu yerleri çoksu urdum bu dağları
Sayvan eyledüm gökleri geri tutup duran benem

Kar yadıran buz konduran hayvanlara rızık veren
Şöyle bilin ol mahluka ol Rahimu Rahman benem

(Yunus Emre, II, p. 205)

> My heart is awakened. I am the one who turns to the face of the Friend.
> I am the one that becomes a river in order to join the sea.
>
> I have overcome the troops of my ego; I have destroyed its towers and fortresses.
> I have cleaned the inside; I am the one who has cleaned the country.
>
> I have faced His Excellency, that Man of Love has opened my eyes.
> He has shown me my own essence; I am the one called *ayet-i kull**

Since the poet believes that God is reflected in everything in the universe, the perfect human being is described both as the power that turns the fire into a rose garden for Abraham and as Nimrod who cast Abraham into the fire, both as Mansur al-Hallaj and as those who punished him.[18]

The number of poems related to Prophet Muhammad, peace and blessings be upon him, and Yunus Emre's approach to his character and that of his Companions in these poems clearly demonstrate that Yunus Emre strictly adheres to the mainstream perception of the Prophet and his Companions. Despite this, there are some contemporary portrayals of Yunus Emre, both in the West and in Turkey, that depict him as a representative of a non-denominational spirituality that makes no reference to his Muslim creed.

Yunus Emre mentions the names of the Prophet and his Companions, including the four caliphs, Abu Bakr, Umar, Uthman and Ali, in numerous places with great respect and reverence. Muham-

---

* *Benüm canum uyanıktır dost yüzüne bakan benem*
Hem denize karışmağa ırmak olup akan benem

Kırdım bu nefsün çerisin bir itdüm burcu barusun
Pak eyledüm içerisin milketini yuyan benem

Ben hazrete tuttum yüzüm ol ışk eri açtı gözüm
Gösterdi bana kendözüm ayet-i küll denen benem

(Yunus Emre, II, pp. 197- 198)

The term *ayet-i küll* in the last line above has various meanings, such as Qur'an, universe, and perfected human being.

mad, peace and blessings be upon him, is the head of the prophets and the final prophet; the whole universe was created because of the love that God has for him.* His features, his compassion for his followers, his moral values, and his *miraj* (ascension to heaven) are mentioned extensively.

> Umar, Uthman and Ali are the Companions of Muhammad
> Of these four, Abu Bakr is the greatest
>
> Abu Bakr and Umar are the great names of the religion.
> Aliyyi Murtaza and Uthman are mine**

Yunus Emre's attitude towards the Prophet and his Companions, especially the four caliphs, leaves no doubt that he follows the mainstream interpretation of the first era of Islamic history. There is not even a single reference to Shiite theology in his poetry.

The poetry of Yunus Emre is not very rich in terms of social criticism, contrary to what some authors, for example, Recep Bilginer,[19] Hasan Kıyafet,[20] or Sebahattin Eyüboğlu,[21] have asserted. There are only a few poems regarding social issues, such as corruption, social justice, and administrative issues. In these poems, the language is very powerful and the criticism is very harsh. Basically, the poet complains that the period in which he lives is the end of time (*akhir zaman*), there is extreme deterioration in all aspects of life, good Muslims are hard to find, scholars do not follow their own advice, the rich exploit the poor, the lines between what is licit and illicit have been lost, the universe is full of corruption, new innovation in reli-

---

* *Yaratdı Hak dünyayı peygamber dostluğuna,*
(Yunus Emre, II, p. 167)

** *Ömer ü Osman Ali Muhammed yarenleri*
Bu dördünün ulusu Ebu Bekri Sıddıkdur
(Yunus Emre, II, p. 100)

Ebu Bekrü Ömer ol din ulusu
Aliyyi Murtaza Osman benümdür
(Yunus Emre, II, p. 48)

gion (*bid'ah*) has replaced the Sunna, the Qur'an is not being followed, the *ulama* have become a burden for the people, etc.[22]

These criticisms are not very significant in terms of showing the social or political aspects of the period. Rather, they are like timeless statements that can be used at any time and for any place. They might be considered disincentives for Sufis, discouraging them from paying attention to the outside world. However, the lack of extensive social criticism in the poetry of Yunus Emre signifies an important aspect of Yunus Emre's thought. As mentioned previously, Yunus Emre aimed to educate the masses and to create a new man in a new land. Without discussing the social issues, Yunus Emre wanted to focus on the individual—the essence of society. This philosophy is beautifully summarized in the following couplet.

> The masses become righteous if you become righteous.
> One cannot find righteousness if you are crooked.*

One of the misconceptions about the poetry of Yunus Emre is that he has a sizeable number of poems about nature.[23] Contrary to this misconception, there are only a few poems in his *Divan* that could be categorized as nature poems. One of the possible reasons for this misconception is the fact that while no comprehensive edition of Yunus Emre's *Divan* was compiled until 1990, the poems have very powerful imagery made up of the elements of nature. Another important factor that creates this impression is the concept of what Annemarie Schimmel calls the cosmic consciousness in Yunus Emre.[24] Since Yunus Emre considers everything in the universe to be a sign of God, he addresses them or gives voice to them.

As said above, although there are only a few poems about nature, there are many powerful images, thus creating the impression that Yunus Emre wrote many poems on nature:

---

* *Cümleler doğrudur sen doğru isen*
Doğruluk bulunmaz sen eğri isen

(Yunus Emre, II, p. 145)

Yunus Emre puns here on the two meanings of the Turkish word *cümle* as "masses" and as "sentences."

My tears flow like a flood, life passes like the wind.
Your smiling face resembles a rose; it does not know that the years are passing.

The nightingale is the beloved of the rose; that is why he is in crying.
His place is the rose garden, he cannot stay in vineyards.*

You have overflowed again! Restless soul, will you splash like the waters?
You are flowing again! My bloody tears, will you block my road?

The snowy mountain opposes my path like a bandit.
I was left separated from my beloved, will you block my road?

The clouds hang in bunches on top of snowy mountains.
Untying your hair, will you cry for me with tears?**

All in all, the thematic classification of the poetry of Yunus Emre makes it clear that in his poetry the main issues are Divine love, death—as an important element that emphasizes the transitory nature of the world—advice, the unity of being, the perfected human being, and the daily prayers. The fact that there are not many poems addressing social issues indicates the basic beliefs of Yunus Emre in particular and of Sufi poetry in general. Yunus Emre believed that the individual human being is the most important element in society and that change and improvement has to start from the individual. The inner world of the individual is represented particularly with the

---

* *Akar yaşım sele benzer ömür geçer yele benzer*
Güler yüzün güle benzer ne bilsün geçe bu çağlar

Gülün bülbül olur yari onunçün kılır zarı
Gülistandır anın yeri makam olmaz ona bağlar

(Yunus Emre, II, p. 73)

** *Taşdun yine deli gönül sular gibi çağlar mısın?*
Akdun yine kanlı yaşım yollarımı bağlar mısın?

Harami gibi yoluma aykırı inen karlı dağ
Ben yarimden ayrı düştüm sen yolumu bağlar mısın?

Karlı dağların başında salkım salkım olan bulut
Saçun çözüp benim için yaşın yaşın ağlar mısın?

(Yunus Emre, II, p. 137)

words for heart (*gönül*, *yürek*, *kalp*), while the relationship between this inner world and God is the most important connection in the entire universe. Exercising love, contemplating death, and reciting didactic poems can help to create the perfected human being who can experience the cosmic consciousness, the presence of God in the universe, and live up to the purpose of the Creation.

An Analysis of the Poems of Yunus Emre

Many of the poems of Yunus Emre portray the experiences and adventures of humankind on the journey to God, that is, on the way to become perfect human beings in a perfect society. In describing these experiences Yunus Emre uses many images and terms from the storehouse of Sufi tradition that had been developed before his time. In his poetry, and that of many others from this tradition, the poet becomes part of the community, as well as the voice of the community. There is a second dimension to this feature that distinguishes these poets as an individual and makes their poetry different and readable; that is, the personal contribution of the specific poet to the tradition. Sufi poetry is liturgical and didactic. However, many Sufis successfully describe their personal experiences in a way that combines both the language of Sufi terminology and their specific personalities. This aspect of Sufi poetry makes it particularly enjoyable to read. Not all poets were able to accomplish this and were unable to free their poetry from becoming an in-group communication tool, a repetition of common Sufi teachings in verse or in a language that can only be understood by those who have knowledge of Sufi tradition.

Yunus Emre was able to accomplish both features in his poetry. His poetry is attractive both to those who are familiar with Sufi tradition and to those who are not.[25] This can be considered to be a strength and beauty of the poetry, and on the poet's part this might be something that was intentionally constructed to attract more readers/listeners, and to bring the ideas to a broader audience.

However, sometimes this feature might lead to interpretations which may not have been desired or acceptable by the poet. One has to know at least the intentions and specific conditions of the poet in order to suggest that any one specific interpretation was that which the poet aimed to create.

Any interpretation can provide some insights as long as it relies on the poetry in question in a way that is not counter to the intentions or purposes of the poet. There are various interpretations of the poetry of Yunus Emre. I have discussed the reasons and motives for these various interpretations in the third chapter. At least, we can say that an interpretation which does not take into consideration the purposes of the poet, or the social and cultural milieu in which the poem was written/recited, should not be presented as if it were what the poet had intended. In the interpretations of Yunus Emre's poetry, intentionally or unintentionally, the methods of New Criticism are predominantly used. In New Criticism, "the poem is an autonomous verbal artifact."[26] The advocates of this theory suggest, "poetry's obligation is not just to convey knowledge but also to be knowledge."[27] For the interpretation of a poem in New Criticism, "knowledge of the poem's language and a good dictionary [are the] only prerequisites."[28] Unfortunately, because of the relatively easy-to-understand language of Yunus Emre and because of reasons that can be considered to be political, such as creating a history for nationalism or denying the Muslim past of Turkish society, the poetry of Yunus Emre has been interpreted without taking into consideration the intentions or background of the poet. The poetry of Yunus Emre is open to different readings; this could be considered to be one of the characteristics of great poetry. However, it is essential to take into consideration the original context in which the poetry was produced. That is to say, this poetry should be evaluated as something that was produced in the 13th and 14th centuries as part of Sufi teachings by a dervish who had a mission in society. The poet is also a man who thinks of himself, and who is considered by the society in which he lived, in a certain way.

I have chosen the following poem to show that understanding the dictionary, literal meanings of the words in the poem does not help us very much and that it is quite difficult to produce a coherent interpretation without considering the philosophical background of the poem. This poem can be considered to be a good representative of the poetry of Yunus Emre, since the style and images are commonly used in his other poems.

1 While I was searching for /contemplating myself, I have reached the astonishing mystery that you too should see in you;
I have seen the Friend in me, brother.

2 I have looked at myself and seen the One who becomes me with me in me.
I have understood who is the One who becomes the soul for my body.

3 I wanted and found Him, if He is me then where am I?
I could not distinguish myself from Him once I became Him, brother!

4 My heart does not obey the one who says the form, the human, is clay.
I caused the essence of this clay to attain God, brother!

5 The unbeliever does not feel this, the souls of those who suffer hurt.
I am the nightingale of the garden of the Friend, I come from that garden, brother.

6 The Beloved (God) is with us all the time; He is not different to each person.
The great length of the road is because of us;
I have found the Friend close, brother.

7 Do not touch me, do not touch or distract me.
This journey has turned out to be a happy one;
I have reached a good place, brother.

8 I was Mansur at that time; I have come again at this time.
Burn me and throw my ashes to the wind; I have said I am the Truth, brother!

9 Neither do I burn in the fire, nor do I become strangled on the gallows.
I will go when my work is done;
I have come here for an excursion, brother.

10 I became the/a Benefactor while I was poor, the whole universe and existence became mine.
I have filled the East and the West, the heavens and the earth completely, O, brother.

11 Eventually, I have come to know myself and I have found the God I desired.
I was fearful until I found Him; I was rescued from fear, brother.

12 Yunus, who kills you, [only] the One who gives takes the sweet soul.
I understood who the One who commands these souls is, brother![29]

When one reads the poetry of Yunus Emre, one of the most important features that catches our attention is the poet's fascination with the "I" (*ben*) or ego. Although Yunus Emre lived at a time in which there was a tremendous amount of social, political, and cultural activity, he hardly mentions any of these. For this reason, his work is not very useful either as a biographical source or as a historical source. It would be safe to say that the poetry of Yunus Emre is not a good mirror for the social reality of the time. Even a basic consideration of the formal aspects of his poems shows his interest in his "I-ness" and his lack of interest in the social events of his age. Out of 416 poems in his *Divan*, around 100 of them are rhymed with the personal pronoun "I" and its derivatives. When we add to this number the poems in which the poet addresses himself in various ways without using the personal pronoun, the total easily reaches 300, which is two-thirds of his entire oeuvre. This might be considered to be an extreme preoccupation with the ego. However, this aspect of Yunus Emre's poetry typically reflects an important and pivotal element in the understanding of Yunus Emre, which is the *wahdat al-wujud* (unity of being), and there are significant reasons for this "obsession" with the ego.

In Sufism in particular and in Islam in general there are two cosmoses reflecting the *sıfat* (attributes) of God: The first one is the microcosm, which is the human being. The second one is the macrocosm, which is the entire universe. In this order, the microcosm is more important than the macrocosm because it is the most comprehensive mirror manifesting the attributes of God in a single entity. In the macrocosm, the attributes of God are spread all around, not condensed as they are in the microcosm.

Like many poems of Yunus Emre, the poem selected for discussion also starts with "I", revealing the understanding that the human being is the microcosm of the universe. Without keeping this understanding in mind, it would be very difficult to provide any sort of meaningful interpretation.

> While I was searching for /contemplating myself,
> I have reached the astonishing mystery that you too should see in you;
> I have seen the Friend in me, brother.

For Sufis, the goal of creation is to know God. All the ritual prayers, all the religious institutions, and all the Prophets and men of God try to teach and facilitate this goal. In a well-known and often repeated hadith qudsi God says, "I was a Hidden Treasure and I desired (loved) to be known; I created the creatures so that I might be known."[30] Sufism is the name of the teaching that offers a method to attain this goal. One can only get to know God by being a perfect human being, one who reflects the attributes of God.

In this process, the microcosm, the "I-ness" (*ben*), becomes extremely important, since it is the most perfect and reachable locus through which God manifests Himself. The microcosm is not the same as the ego or the *nafs* (carnal desires of humans). It has the potential to lead to one becoming a being who is loftier than the angels or lower than the animals. The poet, knowing the importance and potential of "I-ness", starts to contemplate his being, and after going through certain stages, reaches the astonishing mystery: he is able to see and experience the attributes of God in himself. In the second line the poet suggests that people see the same thing in themselves, which is one of the primary functions of Sufi poetry.

In the third couplet the poet discusses the dilemma of Mansur al-Hallaj (d.922), to whom he refers again in the eighth couplet. Mansur al-Hallaj is a famous Sufi who is identified with the celebrated formula of "I am the Truth" (*ana'l Haqq*). He was executed and thrown into a fire for expressing this idea. The gist of Mansur's ideas that led to his death was that since God is reflected in him, there is no point in mentioning the "I" in regards to himself. Even to say "I" while God was within him is considered to be a mistake. Sufis refer to the Qur'an to support this idea, that is, "*Whithersoever you turn, there is the face of God*" (2:115). Hallaj is constantly revered and elevated as the symbol of being a perfect human who paid for this insight with his life. Yunus Emre states this idea in the following couplet:

> I wanted and found Him, if He is me then where am I?
> I could not distinguish myself from Him once I became Him, brother!

In the fourth couplet, Yunus Emre refers to the creation of humankind and Satan's refusing God's order to accept the superiority of Adam, the first human being. In this rejection, Satan's argument was that he had been created from fire, while Adam had been created from clay. From that point on Satan began to try to deflect human beings from the *sirat al-mustaqim* (Straight Path). Yunus Emre states:

> My heart does not obey the one who says the form, the human, is clay.
> I caused the essence of this clay to attain God, brother!

In this couplet, the use of the word heart (*gönül*) is significant. Sufism considers the heart to be the most important faculty of the human being. It is important to bear in mind that although reason is valued too, it is not considered as superior to the heart. In some Sufi texts being intelligent or reasonable is more of a criticism than a compliment. Reason has to be used and has a proper place, but it is not viewed as the most important tool for reaching or finding God. The heart is important because it is the place where God manifests Himself. This is frequently repeated in Yunus Emre's poetry and in other Sufi writings. For Yunus Emre, breaking someone's heart can nullify all the good deeds one has done throughout their life. The Qur'an uses the term "heart" about 130 times to show its significance. A famous hadith qudsi is effective in demonstrating this understanding: "My heavens and My earth embrace Me not, but the heart of My believing servant embraces Me."[31]

Another important element of *wahdat al-wujud* is expressed in the sixth couplet:

> The Beloved (God) is with us all the time; He is not different to each person.
> The great length of the road is because of us; I have found the Friend close by, brother.

Every human being has the potential to reflect the attributes of God, to attain perfection. In a Qur'anic verse, God says, "*We have certainly created the human being in the best stature; then We return him to the lowest of the low*" (95:4–5). Humankind occupies the highest position in creation. However, when it comes to the level of the individual human being, there are many *maratib* (degrees) between being a perfect human being to being the lowest of the low, depending upon how one makes use of what one has and what one is given. In Ibn Arabi's view, "Know that all Divine knowledge by 'immediate tasting,' which is actualized in the people of God, differs from the other according to the differences in the perceptive faculties through which they are actualized, although all this knowledge is ultimately derived from one source."[32] The degrees of individuals are determined according to this knowledge (*marifah*). In his *Futuhat al-Makkiyya* (Meccan Openings), Ibn Arabi explains this idea with two vivid examples. He states, "Just as the one and the same light is colored in various ways as it passes through pieces of glass of various colors, the same Form of the Absolute is manifested differently in different men with different capacities."[33]

The second example Ibn Arabi uses is that of a mirror as a symbol of humankind in relation to God. He states,

> [...] a mirror reflects objects. Sometimes it reflects them as they really are. But in many cases, an object is reflected in a mirror more or less changed or transformed... a large thing appears small in a small mirror, oblong in an oblong mirror and moving in a moving mirror (i.e. running water)[34]

Just like the images in the mirror, the quality and other features of the object are dependent on the position and quality of the mirror, so too are the reflections of the Divine attributes in an individual dependent on the capacity and position of the individual toward God. Yunus Emre states that God, the Object, is not different in the case of each individual. The difference is because of our position; the difference is because of us.

In the 10th couplet, Yunus Emre focuses more on the concept of *wahdat al-wujud*. God, the Necessarily Existent Being, is One in His Essence, His Attributes and His acts; the multiplicity in existence appears through relations between non-essential entities. When discussing the microcosm and macrocosm, I mentioned that the manifestations of God are reflected in both. God's Names and Attributes which have given existence to the whole universe (macrocosm) are manifested in human beings (microcosm) in direct proportion to their submission to God. The degree of this existence reaches a maximum point in the perfect human being. At this point, the attributes of God in the perfect human being and in the universe become identical. Yunus Emre conveys this idea in the following couplet:

> I became the/a Benefactor while I was poor, the whole universe and existence became mine
> I have filled the East and the West, the heavens and the earth completely, O, brother.

In Sufi understanding, everything in the world, every created thing reflects God. Since some Sufis take this point to an extreme degree, they are criticized for blurring the line between good and evil. For example, one of the most prominent Islamic scholars of our time criticizes some Sufis for considering both good and evil to be reflections of God.[35] Sufis explain this by saying that evil is the reflection of certain attributes of God, such as the one who takes revenge (*Muntaqim*). Without going into detail, we can say that it is a well-known and well-established fact that Sufis consider the universe this way. In this understanding, the verse in the Qur'an that says, "*whithersoever you turn, there is the face of God*" (2:115) plays an important role.

In couplet 10, given above, the poet is stating that he became a benefactor while he was a poor and the whole universe thus became his. Both attributes are attributes of God. Thus, in the first line of the couplet there are two terms that are significant: poor and Benefactor. These two terms respectively refer to the starting point and final point on the journey to God (*sayr u suluk*). The poet is describing the transformation of the wayfarer by mentioning two points that are on a single line. *Faqr* (utter poverty) is the position that an ascetic, a wayfarer, should have in relation to God. In order to receive the favors and blessings of God, in order to perfectly reflect the attributes of God, one has to be in utter poverty; that is, the mirror has to be free of any dust or any other material. There is a Qur'anic verse that suggests that alms be given to the poor,[36] which is generally interpreted in relation to the economic regulations of Islam. However, a contemporary of Yunus Emre, the Egyptian Sufi Ibn Ataillah, interprets the verse to mean "if one wants to receive Divine blessings one has to be in utter poverty."[37]

The second significant term in couplet 10, "the Benefactor", is a term attributed to God. When a human being attains perfection, they attain all they want. For Sufis, the most important source of wealth is being with God. As indicated in a well-known hadith, "What is there to lose if one finds God and what is there to gain if one loses God?"[38]

For Sufis, the ultimate goal of human existence is to find and know God. This is the main issue of existence for them. A basic premise of Sufism is that one has to discover and know oneself, since the microcosm is the most perfect and readily available object one can reach. "He who knows himself knows his God" (*man arafa nafsahu faqad arafa Rabbahu*).[39] One question arising at this point is how much can one know oneself and how much can one know one's God? Is it possible to know God absolutely? Sufis say that this is impossible and quote the famous expression by Abu Bakr, the first caliph, who stated: "Incapacity to attain comprehension is itself comprehension."[40] Ibn Arabi states, "...in the view of those who know the self, the self is an ocean without a shore, so knowledge of it has no end."[41]

In the 11th couplet, Yunus Emre states,

> Eventually, I have come to know myself and I have found the God I desired.
> I was fearful until I found Him; I have been rescued from fear, brother.

God is one; He is not different in each person. However, the degrees of knowing Him depend upon the person. As Chittick puts it, "The God that I come to know through knowing myself is the God of my own belief, the water has assumed the color of my cup."[42]

When Yunus Emre states, "I have found the God I desired," he is expressing an idea that is very common in Sufi circles. Rumi mentioned the same idea in his *Mathnawi* with a story. The event in the story takes place during the time of Moses, peace be upon him. Prophet Moses sees a shepherd praying to God as if God were an ordinary human being. Moses warns the shepherd and instructs him how to pray "properly." When Moses talks to God He reproaches Moses, saying that he had prevented one of God's beloved servants from praying to Him as the servant wished.[43]

Throughout the poem, Yunus Emre describes the experiences of a wayfarer on the way to God. The poem starts with the word *sayr*, which means search, or contemplation, and it continues through various stages. The main stages of this poem and the Sufi path are awareness of God's existence in the human heart, the possible distractions on the way, inviting others to the same path, the relief that comes from finding the Object one desires, and freeing oneself of all one's fears.

The Language of Yunus Emre

The language of Yunus Emre has been a controversial issue which has, for the most part, been considered in light of preconceived notions about the poet rather than on the basis of his works. The common perception is that Yunus Emre used a simple Turkish, a Turkish that could be understood by ordinary Turkish-speaking people, both in his own day and in the 20th century. Even the most able scholars, such as Irene Melikoff and Alessio Bombaci,[44] simply repeat the assertion that "Yunus Emre used syllabic meter, which is the meter of folk poetry. [His language] was free from Arabic and Persian loan words, a language with the people and for the people."[45] It is argued that Yunus Emre consciously used the Turkish language rather than Persian and Arabic. I argue that although his language is one of the most important aspects of his poetry, if not the most important one, many presentations of the issue of Yunus Emre's use of Turkish words or how Turkish his language is are simplistic and sometimes statistically wrong.

The idea that Yunus Emre composed his poetry in simple Turkish is repeated by many different people. For İsmet Zeki Eyüboğlu, he "is the poet of people, who spoke Turkish intentionally as opposed to Persian or Arabic; Yunus Emre did not use a language loaded with Arabic and Persian words as the later Ottoman poets did."[46] Trying to prove how Turkish the language of Yunus Emre is, İsmet Zeki Eyüboğlu provides the number of words that Yunus Emre used in specific poems, analyzes the linguistic origins of the words and concludes that Yunus Emre overwhelmingly used words that have a Turkish origin.[47]

Whether the number of words and their linguistic origins make a poem more simple and understandable will be discussed later. However, even this claim is not true. A recent work demonstrates that 49% of the words in Yunus Emre's poetry are Arabic or Persian in origin.[48] When it comes to specific words and expressions, İ. Z. Eyüboğlu argues that Yunus Emre created these elements. He asserts that "although Seljukid and Ottoman poets copied Persian poetry, Yunus Emre was able to stay away from this because of the path he chose."[49]

There is no question that the most important aspect of Yunus Emre's works is his linguistic ability and his ability to express the most complicated issues of Sufism in a very simple and powerfully beautiful language. He is the first and one of the best poets to express the experience of Sufi life and teaching in Turkish. In this regard, Talat Halman is right to call him "the aesthete of ethics";[50] likewise Sezai Karakoç considers Yunus to be the poet who expressed the message of Islam in Turkish and conveyed this message for the perception of the Turks.[51] To explain by using terms borrowed from Noam Chomsky, Yunus Emre was able to express "the mental properties"[52] of the deep structure of Sufism in the Turkish language. If the longing for God is a mental property and has a meaning for human beings, Yunus felt this longing and expressed it in Anatolian Turkish. Mostly because of this linguistic aspect and partly because of the genre that he used, it is highly unlikely that non-Turkish readers would be able to understand and therefore appreciate Yunus Emre as much as native speakers of Turkish do. This might be true for all translated poetry; however, the poetry of a story-telling poet such as Rumi does not get lost in translation to the same extent as other forms of poetry do.

Another important question in regard to the language of Yunus Emre is how ordinary his language is or, as Stanley Fish puts it, "how ordinary ordinary language is."[53] We can rephrase the question: how ordinary or simple is the poetry of Yunus Emre? Add to this another question: Does the fact that ordinary people understand a poem makes it simple? Just because we understand every single word in a so-called modern poem does not mean that we can understand modern poetry easily. How can we be sure that the meaning understood by the so-called ordinary people is the right meaning? One should also consider the fact that "the text is not a line of words releasing a single theological meaning; but a multidimensional space in which a variety of writings, none of them original, blend and clash. The text is a tissue of quotations drawn from the innumerable centers of culture."[54]

The poetry of Yunus Emre, as the multitude of interpretations proves, does not have a single meaning. The interpretations of the same poetry by Annemarie Schimmel and Mehmet Kaplan shed important lights on the work of Yunus Emre, although their interpretation is quite different. While some consider this poetry to be an expression of mystical experience in Turkish, others find elements of an agrarian society which was transformed from a nomadic culture. The poetry of Yunus Emre presents a blend of concepts and quotations from various centers of culture, including the basic source of Islam. There are varying ideas, most of which can also be found in many other Sufi works of the time, such as Rumi, Fakhruddin Iraqi (in poetry) and Ibn Arabi or Qurayshi (in theoretical writings).[55] If one overlooks all of these references and interprets the meaning of the poetry only by depending on the literal meaning of the words, one can only access a single layer of the cultural, historical and personal profoundness of this poetry.

One example of this type of interpretation will shed more light on the discussion. İsmet Zeki Eyüboğlu comments on one of today's most popular poems by Yunus Emre, which says, "Your love has taken me from me / I need You, I need You, / I burn day and night / I need You, I need You." Eyüboğlu states that "we can write these lines and send them to someone who does not have any relation with Sufism, for example a woman. We can assert that (if she does not know Yunus Emre) these lines were written for her."[56]

Another poem in which Yunus Emre suggests that human beings should experience the unity in this world is interpreted as "Yunus Emre wants to experience unity with his friend in this world"[57] as opposed to the next world; this assumption is made because this author assumes that Yunus Emre does not believe in the Hereafter.

The problem with this kind of approach to the language of poems is manifold. Interpreting words which were written in a specific context, at a specific time, and, according to many scholars,[58] for a specific purpose, creates a danger of the meaning being totally distorted. Language or words can only have meaning in relation to objects; signifiers can exist and make sense only as long as they signify something. There is a strong convention in the poetry of Yunus Emre, and in this sense it is very self referential and self-explanatory. One can create another convention and interpret the poetry of Yunus Emre; however, this new text becomes another type of poetry, not that of Yunus Emre. One factor that facilitates this sort of interpretation is that the poetry of Yunus Emre has been simplified in many scholarly and popular works. When compared, one can see the differences between the original version in the manuscript and the published versions. The first comparative edition was made in 1990. There are many examples of this kind of simplification in Gölpınarlı's edition,[59] which help to create a false impression that the language of Yunus Emre was purely Turkish and easily understandable.

Chapter 3

Reception of Yunus Emre

RECEPTION OF YUNUS EMRE

Reception Theory/Reader Response Criticism

Namık Kemal, (1840–1888) the novelist, poet and activist of the Tanzimat era, narrates the following anecdote:

> I don't remember exactly what year it was, but it must have been 1278 AH [1861 CE]. One day during the month of Ramadan, I went to the booksellers in the courtyard of Sultan Beyazıt mosque to look for books. They gave me a piece of paper in the *taliq* style and asked for 20 *para*. I paid the money and bought the paper. I saw the title of *ilahi* [a genre of Ottoman poetry] and thought that it was a dervish Yunus *ilahi*. I started to read it anyway. That *ilahi*... Do you know what it was?[1]

Namık Kemal continues to explain that it was not by Yunus, but Şinasi (1826–1871), one of the pioneers of Westernization in Turkey, and praises him for his contributions to intellectual development and to the simplification of the Turkish literary language.

This passage is significant in two aspects: The first aspect is that Ottoman intellectuals were aware of Yunus Emre and his work, as will be discussed in the following section on the reception of Yunus Emre during the Ottoman period. The second aspect of this anecdote is that Ottoman/Turkish intellectuals were looking for a new way to express themselves, and the West was their ultimate model. In this chapter, the question that I am trying to answer is what had changed between the time of Namık Kemal and the time of Fuat Köprülü that made them perceive the poetry of Yunus Emre so differently. The poetry of Yunus Emre was definitely available and well known by Ottoman intellectuals. What changed so drastically to cause Turkish intellectuals to develop a keen interest in Yunus Emre? The answers to these questions are closely related to the reception of Yunus Emre in the 20th century. In answering this and related questions I will use reader response criticism and reception theory.

There are various reasons why the poetry of Yunus Emre is attractive to so many people, while at the same time it is the center of many different and sometimes contradictory perspectives. There is no doubt that Yunus Emre is the most controversial poet in Turkish literature as far as the variety of interpretations of his poetry and the groups who claim him as their own are concerned. In analyzing these interpretations and the factors that contribute to these results, reception theory/reader response criticism is very helpful and provides a useful framework for analysis. Certain terms that are provided by reader response criticism and its emphasis on the reader as the maker of meaning are especially helpful in understanding scholarship on Yunus Emre. Indeterminacies and their role in the making of meaning and the effect of interpretive communities are also two important elements in reader response criticism which provide fruitful results in understanding the reception of Yunus Emre.

In this work, I will use reader response criticism / reception theory to analyze both the scholarly and popular reception of the poetry of Yunus Emre as this will provide a productive analytical framework. The roots of reader response criticism and reception theory can be traced back to Aristotle and Plato, who discussed the impact of literary works on readers. In the 20th century, various literary theories, especially those of the French structuralists and feminists, have dealt extensively with the issue of the impact of a work on the reader. The most important component of these theories is that they consider the reader to be of central importance in the creation of meaning.

Although born independently and in different places reader response criticism and reception theory share similar principles and are considered to be complementary to one another. Reception theory was born and widely discussed in Western Europe, specifically Germany, whereas reader response criticism was formulated in North America. In particular, reader response criticism was a reaction to New Criticism. New Criticism takes the literary work as an object that is independent of its author. As T. S. Eliot argues, "honest criticism and sensitive appreciation are directed not upon the poet, but upon the poetry."[2] Among the scholars who are included in these two schools of criticism are Wolfgang Iser, Jonathan Culler, E. D. Hirsch, David Bleich, Stanley Fish, Norman Holland and Hans Robert Jauss.

I will briefly summarize the most important elements of the schools that will be used in this work. Both reader response criticism and reception theory consider the reader to be an important element in creating the meaning of a work. They argue that a book on the shelf or a text on the page has no meaning without the reader. Once a reader becomes involved, the process of making meaning starts. The process continues with the participation of the reader. For this reason, the reader must be considered an imperative element of a literary work. Jauss argues that we can understand literary work by analyzing the role of the reader in the process of creating meaning. Norman Holland takes this suggestion one step further and argues that readers recreate their own identity through their response to literary texts. Some scholars, such as David Bleich, leave no room for the text and consider the meaning of a literary work to be entirely a function of the reader's personality.[3]

In these two theories, in the process of making sense of the text, or creating meaning, what the reader expects from the text becomes very important, since what the reader expects and the meaning of the text have a very strong correlation. A reader approaches a text with a set of expectations. This set of expectations is called "the horizon of expectations," a key term in these schools of criticism. A reader constructs the meaning according to what they expect from the text being read. The fact that the same text is interpreted differently at different times proves the validity of this idea.

For example, Jauss argues that since the horizons of expectation change over time, the literary work offers different interpretations in different historical periods.[4]

In determining the meaning, interpretive communities, that is, individuals who share similar thoughts and expectations, become an important factor. Academic communities, religious institutions, and political groups have certain principles that make them a group and this similarity can also be observed in their approach to a given text. These groups share strategies to understand and interpret a text. Fish argues that, "these strategies exist prior to the act of reading and therefore determine the shape of what is read rather than, as is usually assumed, the other way around."[5] These strategies do not make the preexisting meaning of the text because, according to Fish, meaning is not in the text at all.

One of the most criticized aspects of reader response and reception theory is the extreme emphasis on the personal preferences of the reader. If any reader has the right to inject their own meaning as the right meaning for the text, this takes interpretation to a point where there is no point of reference left, other than that of the reader. To balance this absolute relativism, reader response critics argue that the freedom of the reader in interpretation is not random. Readers make interpretations by filling in the gaps (blanks) or indeterminacies. The amount of indeterminacies not only allows the readers to join the meaning-making process, but also makes the text difficult to read.[6] As long as the reader tries to understand the meaning of the text by filling in the blanks with referral to external variable factors, then these indeterminacies can serve aesthetic purposes and in no way should they be considered to be a defect.[7]

The last important element of these two theoretical approaches is their attitude towards literary history and the function of literary works in society. German literary critic Jauss deals with this issue extensively in his *Aesthetic Experience and Literary Hermenutics*.[8] Jauss probes a literary historiography that plays a conscious, mediating role between past and present. He also proposes that art can play a progressive and affirmative role.

The reason that I have chosen to use reader response criticism and reception theory is that the poetry of Yunus Emre has many interpretations and most, if not all, of these interpretations are in line with the political and ideological views of their interpreters. In this case, the most important dynamic in the interpretation is the reader. I looked for a literary theory that will provide tools for analyzing the importance and position of the reader. Reader response criticism and reception theory were chosen because they deal primarily with this issue.

A brief historical categorization of the interpretations of the poetry and biography of Yunus Emre shows that interpretations correlate with contemporary political trends in Turkish society and with the ideology of the interpreters. Fuat Köprülü, who is considered to be the founder of Turkish cultural nationalism, is an example of interpretation that can be related to politics. Köprülü explicitly states that he was looking for something that could prove the literary genius of the Turkish nation and found this in Yunus Emre at a time when nationalism was on the rise. In other words, Köprülü's interpretation of the poetry of Yunus Emre is very much related to his own ideology rather than Yunus Emre or the poetry.

People who share similar thoughts with Köprülü formed an interpretive community, but there are other interpretive communities as well. These communities also interpret Yunus Emre from their own perspectives rather than the poet's. In some of these interpretations, it is very easy to see the affect of the time of the interpretation and the lack of a historical or textual base. An interesting example is the discussions over whether Yunus Emre was a Bektashi or not. In order to prove that he was not a Bektashi, literary historian Ahmet Kabaklı interprets the word *Tapduk* not as a personal name, which is certainly the case, but as a name for God, which makes it impossible for Yunus to be a Bektashi.[9] Kabaklı's interpretation is motivated by the political circumstances of Turkey during the 1970s and early 1980s and the interpretive and political community to which he belongs. In the 1970s and 1980s, Bektashis were associated with leftist ideologies and Kabaklı did not want to see Yunus Emre as a Bektashi.

The most intriguing element of reader response criticism and reception theory in the case of Yunus Emre is the idea of indeterminacies and how they shape the reception of his poetry. In the case of Yunus Emre, there are indeterminacies on three levels: textual, historical, and cultural.

Until 1990, there was no comprehensive edition of the works of Yunus Emre and this caused any consideration of his works to be only partial. Because all of his poems were not readily available before 1990, some authors assumed that his language was easily understandable or some authors described him as a poet who composed a considerable amount of poems about nature, although only a few of his 416 poems can be called poems about nature.[10]

On the historical level, there is little reliable information about the biography of Yunus Emre. The period and geography in which Yunus Emre lived is one of the murkiest times and places in Turkish history. It is also the meeting point of many various religions, sects, ethnicities, and socio-political activities. This is also a time at which many boundaries, whether ethnic, tribal, sectarian or religious, were broken and blurred. The transformation and interconnectedness of the institutions and the lack of historical documents about the biography of Yunus Emre create more uncertainties.

On the cultural level, the cultural milieu of Yunus Emre is naturally very different from the 20th century. The language used by Yunus Emre with its terminological usages and connotations is extremely difficult for a 20th century reader to penetrate. Although some of his poems seem easy to understand, this is true only on the surface level of the language; this simplicity fails to provide a good picture of his philosophy. Another issue that makes the poetry of Yunus Emre difficult is the lack of knowledge of the philosophical aspect of Islam. Many scholars and popular authors try to understand and explain Yunus Emre without considering his era and background.[11] The gaps have been filled in with elements that were foreign to Yunus Emre, whether it is 20th century Turkish nationalism or Western humanism.

As discussed in the introduction, there is not much reliable information about the life of Yunus Emre. All scholars unanimously accept this. The grand master of the Turkish archives, Ali Emiri Efendi (1857–1924), even criticizes the publication of Fuat Köprülü's monograph on Yunus Emre by questioning how one can write a book about a person about whom we know so little.[12]

The second indeterminacy is the cultural gap that was created during the modernization/Westernization period, which started in the late Ottoman and early Republican periods and has continued to this day. Until the 19th century Sufism in particular and Islam in general were inherent parts of Turkish society. Even a brief analysis of the Turkish language gives an idea about how widespread Sufism was. A book by Gölpınarlı about proverbs, idioms, and expressions that originated from Sufism is only one example.[13] If we ask the question of what is signified in Yunus Emre's poetry, we have to consider the most important three elements to be his understanding of the universe, which can be summed up as Sufism, the social conditions of his time, and his personality.

At this point, to answer the question of "what does the poetry of Yunus Emre signify," or to fill in the gaps that occur at numerous levels of the text, it would be helpful to turn to the issue of interpretive communities. One of the factors that increased the number of interpretive communities in Yunus Emre's case is his language, which is relatively easy to understand; however, in some ways this simplistic language only makes the matter of analyzing his interpretive communities more complicated. If one were to use the Saussaurian terms,[14] namely, signifier and signified, it would be safe to say that in Yunus Emre's modern interpretations, the signifier, the poems or the words, have stayed the same, but what they signify has changed. There are historical and cultural reasons for this phenomenon.

In Turkey, in order to create a "pure Turkish language" the words that were considered to be of Arabic and Persian origins were replaced with made up words or borrowings from other Turkic languages or local dialects.[15] Today, there are two terms for the Turkish language: Turkish (*Türkçe*) and Ottoman (*Osmanlıca*), and many people seriously believe that Ottoman is a different language. In this sense, the advocates of the language revolution in Turkey have been successful in being able to create the Ottomans as the "other," and Ottoman Turkish as the language of the "other." In Yunus Emre's case, the signifier is there, but what it signifies has changed due to the cultural gap created by the nationalist policies that were introduced in most domains of Turkish life.

Reception and Impact of Yunus Emre in the Ottoman Period

The analyses of the reception of Yunus Emre before the 19th century provides us with significant information on the popularity of his poetry and it shows how this interpretation in the Ottoman period was different from that of modern interpretations of the poetry of Yunus Emre. Although there are abundant historical and literary sources on this subject, they have not received much attention. Analyzing the reception of Yunus Emre and his poetry in the Ottoman period and comparing it with more modern interpretations will provide illuminating results both for the scholarship of Yunus Emre and other larger issues, such as the division of literary milieus, the division of Sufi brotherhoods, and to a certain degree, the use of literary works in the history-making process in the 20th century.

First, information from this period about Yunus Emre will be provided that demonstrates that Yunus Emre was well known and commonly read/recited in the Ottoman period not only among a specific literary milieu such as the Sufi brotherhoods, or in certain strata of society, but by various literary milieus, Sufi groups, and at different levels of society.[16]

The first source that provides us with significant information about Yunus Emre is the *Vilayetname*, which is attributed to Hacı Bektaş Veli.[17] As legend has it, and as narrated in the *Vilayetname*, Yunus Emre was a farmer in the northern part of Sivrihisar, a small town in today's central Turkey, and he made a living planting crops. One year there was a famine and Yunus Emre went to Hacı Bektaş to acquire wheat. He took some wild plums as a gift for Hacı Bektaş. He went to Hacı Bektaş's house, stayed there for some time, and when it was time for him to leave Hacı Bektaş asked him whether he wanted to take wheat with him or a spiritual blessing (*nefes*). Yunus Emre insisted on the wheat. Eventually, he took the wheat and left for his village. On the way to his village, he understood the mistake he had made and went back to Hacı Bektaş, but unfortunately it was too late and Hacı Bektaş told him that he had given the key for his spiritual nourishment to Tapduk Emre.

Yunus then found Tapduk Emre and explained the situation. Tapduk Emre admitted him to the "service." Yunus started bringing firewood from the forest for the dervish lodge (*tekke*). He never brought any damp or crooked wood to the *tekke*. For forty years he continued to work like this. One day, the dervishes and the spiritual leader, Tapduk Emre, wanted to hear a hymn from a person called Yunus-i Güyende, but he could not recite it. Then Tapduk Emre turned to Yunus Emre and wanted him to recite. Whatever Yunus Emre said became "pearls" and his words became his poetry.

Another much used source of information about Yunus Emre is Aziz Mahmud Hüdayi's (d.1628) *Waqıat*.[18] According to this work, Yunus Emre worked for thirty years in the service of Tapduk Emre. He carried so much wood from the forest that his back became sore, but still he did not complain. Yunus Emre's teacher liked him so much that the other dervishes in the *tekke* (dervish lodge) became jealous. Because he served loyally and without any complaint they started the rumor that he was in love with the daughter of his master. Eventually, Tapduk came to hear of this. One day Yunus brought wood to the *tekke*, and Tapduk asked why he always brought straight wood. Yunus said, "The one who is not righteous (straight) does not belong here." The dervishes had started the rumors not because they had ill intentions, but rather because Yunus was doing something that was beyond human capacity. The teacher knew Yunus's situation and he had no doubts about Yunus.

Eventually, in order to save the other dervishes from being liars, Tapduk gave his daughter's hand in marriage to Yunus. Yunus said he did not deserve such a wife because while this girl was reciting the Qur'an, running waters would stop and listen to her.

In some legends we see Yunus Emre leaving the dervish lodge to look for other ways of spiritual perfection. According to one legend, after serving his master for thirty years, Yunus still could not get what he wanted, i.e. the attainment of spiritual perfection. Therefore, he ran away and went to travel across various mountains and valleys. One day he met seven dervishes in a cave. Every night one of them would pray and food would fall from the sky in answer to their prayers. When it was Yunus' turn he prayed, too. That night twice as much food fell. They asked Yunus for whom he had prayed but he asked them to tell him first. They said that they were praying for a dervish who served Tapduk Emre for thirty years. When Yunus heard this he realized that he was the person to whom they were referring. With this, he returned to the *tekke*. The spiritual master said to him: "You came back after discovering your rank, did you not?"

Aşık Çelebi (d.1571) in his *Mashairu'sh-Shuara* refers to Yunus Emre as a rare perfect human being (*insan al-kamil*). He also mentions that Yunus Emre was illiterate, that he wanted to learn how to read and write but could not, and that he spoke with the language of disposition (*hal dili*), not with his tongue.[19]

Mehmed Said Efendi (d.1802), who was a sheikh in the Gülşeni order, writes the following in his *Mecmua* (*Collection*):[*] "We heard from our ancestors that Yunus Emre would pray this way and it would be accepted. It was recorded here for blessing:

Oh! One God with one thousand and one names,
Oh The All-Glorified! With one hundred thousand names
There is a difficulty; we need a remedy,
Oh! All-Compassionate, You help us!

Yunus Emre would reply in this way if someone asked for a prayer and it would be accepted."

Sheikh Süleyman Efendi of Köstendi (d.1819) mentions Yunus, his master, his poetry, and his endeavors to bring wood to the *tekke* in his *Bahru'l-Walaya*,[20] a book of saints. This text provides the following information, "It is narrated that Rumi said: 'Whichever Divine stations I have attained, I have found the footsteps of an elderly Turkmen. I could not pass him.' The person that he referred to was Yunus Emre."[21]

Other than the written sources provided above, there is plenty of information about Yunus Emre that can be collected from oral sources which show that Yunus Emre was well known in various parts of society.[22] A man named Mullah Qasim read the poetry of Yunus Emre. He found the first one thousand poems offensive and burned them; he found the second one thousand poems offensive too and threw them into the water; when he came to the 2001st poem, he read the following couplet:

---

* *Binbir adlu bir Allah*
Yüzbin adlu ya Subhan
Bir iş düştü bir derman
Sen yarı kıl ya Rahman

(Gölpınarlı, *Yunus Emre ve Tasavvuf*, p. 57)

Oh dervish Yunus, don't tell this word in a bent or crooked (devious) way
A Mullah Qasim comes and questions you*

When Mullah Qasim read this, he was surprised; he repented and began to believe in the sainthood of Yunus Emre, but now there was only one thousand poems left, out of three thousand. It is believed that the fish read the poems Mullah Qasim had thrown into the water, the angels read the poems he had burned, and that people read the poems that were left.

Whether Yunus Emre and Rumi ever met is a controversial issue. An oral source provides us with the following story: Yunus met Rumi and asked if he had written the *Mathnawi*, the six-volume magnum opus of Rumi, and Rumi responded, "Yes." Yunus then said, "You have written too much. If I were you I would say:

I wrapped myself with flesh and bone
I've appeared as Yunus

and this would be sufficient."**

Important issues which should be discussed in regard to these legends include analyses of the legends, the reception of Yunus in these sources, and the relationship of this information with the other Sufi, especially Bektashi, *tariqas*.

To date, these legends have been mostly analyzed from a historical point of view. Certainly, it is important to analyze the language of these legends, both from literary and historical perspectives. However, a historical analysis alone would not bring many insights to the topic. Some scholars, for instance, discuss the legend that refers to a meeting between Rumi and Yunus and conclude

---

* Derviş Yunus bu sözü eğri büğrü söyleme
Seni sigaya çeken bir Molla Kasım gelir
(Gölpınarlı, Yunus Emre ve Tasavvuf, p. 60).

** Ete kemiğe büründüm
Yunus diye göründüm
(Gölpınarlı, Yunus Emre ve Tasavvuf, p. 61).

that this is historically not true.[23] From a literary perspective, this is not the most important issue. We may lack proof of the legend's veracity, but it nevertheless provides important information regarding the imagination of people in Anatolia, who make this connection. In the Anatolian people's minds, Yunus and Rumi came together, thus undermining the idea that there were strict distinctions between various brotherhoods.

We should also consider the symbolic nature of the language of the legends. The wild plums in the legend that Yunus Emre took to Hacı Bektaş can be viewed literally as fruit, or symbolically as an uneducated, uncultivated, or spiritually deficient person. Again, in the same legend, Yunus' carrying of straight wood to the *tekke* for forty years could be interpreted as a fact, or as bringing righteous disciples to the dervish lodge over a long period. Some legends, such as leaving the dervish lodge and returning after finding out its importance, or of boiling in a pot for three days are also attributed to Hacı Bektaş Veli with minor changes in his *Vilayetname*.[24]

One important reason why Yunus Emre is considered to be a forerunner of Turkish cultural nationalists is the way these legends are interpreted. There is a strong understanding that Yunus Emre was Bektashi. Since the interpretations of the legends attributed to Hacı Bektaş are very nationalistic in character, the interpretation of the poetry of Yunus Emre is colored by this understanding. The *Vilayetname* is one of the most important books of the Bektashi order, if not the most. What the *Mathnawi* is to Mawlawis the *Vilayetname* is to the Bektashis. As mentioned earlier, there are two modern editions of the *Vilayetname,* one by Gölpınarlı and one by Bedri Noyan. The interpretations of two legends by Noyan in the introduction to his edition of the *Vilayetname* are striking in terms of showing the state of mind that is employed to interpret the works of Hacı Bektaşı Veli and Yunus Emre. In the *Vilayetname*, we have the following two legends: "One day when Hacı Bektaş was sitting on a wall or on a stone in front of his dervish lodge, he saw that another Sufi, riding a lion, was approaching. Seeing this

Hacı Bektaş ordered the wall or stone to move, and it did. When he came close to the dervish, Hacı Bektaş said 'Anyone can move a living creature. What is important is to move a dead thing.'"[25]

In another legend about the animation of stones, Hacı Bektaş was taking care of the cows in a village. Somebody came and wanted him to take care of his animals too. Hacı Bektaş did not accept this responsibility, but the man left his cows anyway and went home. At the end of the day, the man's cows were eaten by wolves. The man wanted to hold Hacı Bektaş responsible, and claimed that Hacı Bektaş had promised to take care of his animals. At this time, the stones started to speak and testified that Hacı Bektaş was not responsible for the dead cows.[26] In both legends the idea is that a man of faith can communicate and utilize the elements in the universe by using his spiritual power, which is very common in hagiographies.[27]

Bedri Noyan interprets the first legend as "giving life to dead Turkishness" and the second one as "Hacı Bektaş wanting to give a voice to the Turkish language, to Turkishness, by making the stones speak. The situation of Turkish and Turkishness were just like these dead stones at the time."[28] This is nothing but applying a 19th or 20th century phenomenon to the world of the 13th century. Certainly prior to the 19th century, these legends meant to show the spiritual power of the saint, not his beliefs regarding the Turkish language.

Having discussed some of the best-known legends, I will now explore the reception of Yunus Emre in the context of parallel poems (*nazira*), commentaries (*sharh*), and music in the Ottoman period. There are some scholars who use other criteria to show the reception of Yunus Emre. Among these criteria, the most commonly used element is influence. Gölpınarlı and Mustafa Tatçı provide many examples that are intended to show the influence of Yunus Emre in later centuries. Since influence is a subjective and debatable issue, and as the question of whether a certain style belongs to an individual or period has no clear answer, I will avoid using it. Rather, I will use parallel poems and commentaries, primarily because they have an organic relationship with the poetry for which they were written. The *nazira*s and *sharh* are the most valuable sources through which we can trace the reception of Yunus Emre without raising the problem of subjectivity.

Composing parallel poems or *nazira* is a poetic tradition common in Turkish, Persian, and Arabic literature. It is the writing of a poem that is very similar to another poem; that is to say, a poet takes a well-known and appreciated poem and attempts to create a new poem of equal or higher poetic value in the same meter, rhyme, and theme. It is a challenge, a competition, and a commentary. The poet of a *nazira* [*nazire* in Turkish] in a way is suggesting that they are building upon and continuing a tradition. The *nazira* tradition is also important in terms of inter-textuality. The poets of *nazira* use the advantages of the original poem, and in a way take advantage of the aesthetic aura created by the original poem. It is a way of communication between the texts and poets across centuries and cultures, even across languages. The parallel poem has various names, depending upon how the additional lines have been added or whether a single language or more than one language is involved in the composition of the poem.[29]

The second source material to be used is commentaries (*sharh*). As the name signifies, commentaries are texts that explain the poems. In the Turkish case, the author of a commentary, implicitly or explicitly, suggests that they have a superior knowledge of the poem in question than others, and therefore they have the authority to explain it. One common feature in parallel poems and commentaries is that there are very few parallel poems or commentaries that are critical of the original work. Writing commentaries or parallel poems on a work almost always indicates that the commentator or the poet of parallel poem likes and appreciates the poem. The second issue for both commentaries and parallel poems is that there must be a demand for these works and people must know the original works very well. They have to be canonical in the literary milieu so that a poem written about another poem becomes a poem written about a famous poem.

Parallel Poems

The first person known to have written parallel poems for Yunus Emre's poems was Said Emre in the 14th century; according to Gölpınarlı, Said Emre translated Hacı Bektaş' *Maqalat* (Essays) from Arabic into Turkish. In many cases, his poems were confused with Yunus Emre's and included in Yunus' *Divan*.[30]

The second poet to write parallel poems in the same century for Yunus is Ahmedi (d.1412–1413), who is considered to be one of the founders of Divan literature. We can see great similarities between Yunus Emre and Ahmedi. The two poems that are given here show this great similarity in particular:

> Your love has taken me from me, what I need is You, You
> I have been burning day and night, what I need is You, You
> Neither do I become happy for being rich nor do I feel sorry for being poor
> I feel content with Your love, what I need is You You[31]
>
> Yunus Emre

> I am tired of the world, what I need is You, You
> I am worn out by people, what I need is You, You
>
> What will I do with a body and a soul, what I need is You, You
> What will I do with religion and belief, what I need is You, You[32]
>
> Ahmedi

It is impossible not to see the relationship between these two poems in terms of the parallel use of images, expressions, and understandings of religious concepts. The poem for which Ahmedi writes a parallel is one of the best-known and most often-repeated poems of Yunus Emre, and demonstrates the dominant features of his poetic style. The *redif* (repeated expression) of "*Bana seni gerek seni*," "What I need is You, You," at the end of each couplet is apparent in both poems. The idea of rejecting worldly rewards, indeed, going one step further and rejecting other worldly rewards, for the sake of God and emphasizing that the most important thing is the love of God, not the fear of hell or the hope of heaven, is common in both poems and are the main elements of the poetry of Yunus Emre. This similarity and the fact that Ahmedi is considered to be one of the founders of Divan literature calls into question the validity of the idea that Divan literature in the late 14th and early 15th the century and the poetry of Yunus Emre were very different from each other; this is a twentieth century idea, expressed by many literary historians and critics, including Köprülü.

In the 15th century, Abdullah Rumi (d.1469), also known as Eşrefoğlu or Eşrefzade,[33] the founder of the Eşrefiyye, which is a branch of Qadiriyya brotherhood, was an important follower of Yunus Emre in poetry. His poem that starts with the following couplet:

> I need to tell what should be done for those who are on the way of the Friend
> With whom should be friends and whom they should leave*

is a poetic parallel of Yunus Emre's poem that starts with the following couplet:

> Come! Oh! The one who wants to become a dervish; I will tell you what to do
> One should leave the sweet drink and drink the poison**

In the 16th century the founder of the Gülşeniyya brotherhood, which is a branch of the Halwatiyya, İbrahim Gülşeni[34] (d.1533–1534), wrote parallel poems for Yunus Emre's poems.

---

* *Dost yoluna gidenlere aydam ona nitmek gerek*
Kimin ile yoldaş olup kimleri terk etmek gerek
(Gölpınarlı, *Yunus Emre ve Tasavvuf*, p. 213)

** *Gel ey dervişlik isteyen eydem sana nitmek gerek*
Şerbetü elinden koyup aguyu nuş itmek gerek
(Gölpınarlı, *Yunus Emre ve Tasavvuf*, p. 214)

Death has come and bent my back; I have opened my hands to You, God
I have deviated from the path, I have opened my hands to You, God
İbrahim Gülşeni

You are the All-Gracious, You are the All-Merciful, I have opened my hands to You God
I have no cure other than You, I have opened my hands to You God
Yunus Emre*

Shah Ismail of the Safavid dynasty[35] (d.1524), who was the famous rival of the Ottoman Sultan Yavuz Selim I (1470–1529) and used Hatayi as his poetic pseudonym, composed a number of parallel poems for Yunus Emre's poems. In one of his parallel poems, he changes the word "O" (He) to Ali, which is a striking example of how he used poetry to express his Shiite beliefs and to advocate his political views. While Yunus wrote:

I love You more than my soul
I cannot pass beyond this path**

Shah Ismail altered it by writing:

I love Ali more than my soul
I love his path more than any other***

---

* *Ecel erüp bükdü belim Allah sana sundum elüm*
Sağ u sola sapıp yolum Allah sana sundum elüm
İbrahim Gülşeni

Sensün kerim sensün rahim Allah sana sundum elüm
Senden artık yoktur emüm Allah sana sundum elüm
(Gölpınarlı, *Yunus Emre ve Tasavvuf*, p. 216)

** *Severem ben seni candan içeri*
Yolum ütmez bu erkandan içeri
(Yunus Emre, II, p. 294)

*** *Ali'yi severem candan içerü*
Yolunu severem yoldan içerü
(Gölpınarlı, *Yunus Emre ve Tasavvuf*, p. 238)

Hatayi composed other *naziras* for well-known poems of Yunus Emre. I will provide only two more examples here:

> The word makes the person happy, who knows how to use it
> The word makes the affairs of the person better, who masters the word before saying it
> There are words that end the war, there are words that kill the person
> There are words that turn a poisonous meal into honey and butter[36]
>
> The word makes the person who tells it consistently
> The word makes someone honest, who follows the word of the spiritual teacher
> There is a word among people; there is word even in creation
> Do not utter a crooked word so that you will not have to fall into a delicate situation[37]

Sinan Ümmi (d.1551) is another poet who composed parallel poems for Yunus Emre's poems in the 16th century. His poem that starts with:

> *Erenlerin sohbeti ele giresi değil*
> *İkrar ile girenler mahrum kalası değil*[38]
>
> ("It is difficult to find conversation (*sohbet*) with perfect human beings
> Those who enter by faith are not deprived.")

is a parallel poem for Yunus Emre's poem that starts with:

> *Mani eri bu yolda melul olası değül*
> *Mani tuyan gönüller hergiz ölesi değül*[39]
>
> ("The men of true meaning do not regret being on this path
> The souls that feel the true meaning do not perish at all.")

The founder of the Jalwatiyya brotherhood, Üftade[40] (d.1580–1581), was also influenced by Yunus Emre and made references to and quoted Yunus in his conversations in *Waqıat*, a book written by his disciples and composed of his words.[41] Üftade's disciple, Aziz Mahmud Hüdayi (d.1624–1625), was the most important follower of Yunus Emre in the 17th century in the realm of poetry. He wrote a number of parallel poems for Yunus Emre's poems.[42] Another important name in this century was Niyazi Mısri[43] (d.1694), who wrote many parallel poems for Yunus Emre's poems and a famous commentary, which I will discuss later. Mısri wrote a parallel poem, which started with the following couplet:

> You wish for the friends without leaving the ignorant people
> You wish to become a human being without abandoning being an animal*

This corresponds to Yunus Emre's poem that starts with the following couplet:

> You have not left your own desire behind and you want the Beloved
> You have not cut the rope girdle and wish for belief**

Another poet of the 17th century, Nakhshi-i Akkirmani (d.1651–1652) also composed parallel poems for Yunus Emre:

> I am an orphan pearl that appears as a human being
> The whole universe is at my order and the universe is hidden in my atom***
>
> Nakhshi-i Akkirmani

> I am an orphan pearl which the ocean has not seen
> I am a drop, but I am the ocean for the ocean****
>
> Yunus Emre

---

* *Nadanı terketmeden yaranı arzularsın*
Hayvanı sen geçmeden insanı arzularsın
(Gölpınarlı, *Yunus Emre ve Tasavvuf*, p. 228)

** *Sen canından geçmedin canan arzu kılarsın*
Belden zünnar kesmedin iman arzu kılarsın
(Gölpınarlı, *Yunus Emre ve Tasavvuf*, p. 228)

*** *Bir dürr-i yetimem ki geldüm görünüp insane*
Emrimde kamu derya zerremde cihan pinhan
(Gölpınarlı, *Yunus Emre ve Tasavvuf*, p. 228)

**** *Bir dürr-i yetimem ki görmedi beni umman*
Bir katreyim illa ki ummana benim umman
(Gölpınarlı, *Yunus Emre ve Tasavvuf*, p. 228)

Mahvi İsa, (d.1715) who was a member of the Gülşeniyya brotherhood and a judge in Damascus, composed parallel poems for Yunus Emre's famous riddle-like poem (Niyazi Mısri also wrote a commentary for this poem).[44]

All these works, plus many others, demonstrate that Yunus Emre was being read and appreciated continuously during the Ottoman period. It is groundless to claim that Yunus Emre was not appreciated as a poet in the Ottoman period. We see that there is a strong chain of continuity from the 14th to the 19th century and that the final links of the chain appear to be much stronger than the earlier ones. This is primarily because of the availability of sources, particularly from the oral tradition and music, in the later centuries.

The first conclusion we can draw from the written legends and other written sources is that Yunus Emre's poetry was read and widely appreciated by poets and Sufi leaders during the Ottoman period. However, in these sources Yunus Emre is referred to as a dervish, an *arif* (sage), a saint, an *insan al-kamil* (perfect human being), but rarely as poet. Based on the sources that we have, it would not be wrong to suggest that, at least for the Sufis, poetry, although important, definitely came second to being a man of God or an *insan al-kamil*. Poetry was a tool that could be used for devotional or didactic purposes. Otherwise, it does not seem to have had any significant value of its own. In other words, it was a means to communicate a message, not an end in itself.

The commentary of Niyazi Mısri provides an important example of the idea that the poetry is supposed to convey a message. Niyazi Mısri, according to his own account,[45] wrote his commentary on a poem of Yunus Emre and waited for some time before sharing it with others. One day, he saw Yunus Emre in a dream or vision, and Yunus Emre told him to change a certain part and let other people read the commentary. This account shows that the poem itself was not the most important thing when it came to interpretation, in contrast to what some modern critics have suggested. The work is not independent of its creator, and there is a fixed meaning that is directly related to the poet or the author.

It is very clear that Yunus Emre's poems were appreciated in the Ottoman period, and his style was praised for both its semantic and aesthetic value. However, there is hardly any mention of the aesthetic value of his poetry by the authors of the commentaries. We can say that his dervish character overshadows his artistic endeavors; there are not many references to the aesthetic value of his poetry, although Yunus Emre is the primary representative of popular mystical poetry and his poetry did have a following, as the *naziras* and commentaries prove.

The second conclusion that we can draw from the legends, parallel poems, and collections of conversations (*sohbet mecmuası*) is that a wide range of groups, from Mevlevis to Bektashis and from Halwatis to Qadiris, embraced the poetry of Yunus Emre. Certainly it is very important to try to determine the specific brotherhood to which Yunus Emre belonged, however, it would not be incorrect to say that the poetry of Yunus Emre was welcomed and accepted by many brotherhoods, such as Bektashi, Nakhshi, Qadiri, Gülşeni, Malami and Halwati, as indicated by the poets who composed parallel poems for Yunus Emre's poetry.

The fact that Yunus Emre was accepted by such a diversity of *tariqas* calls into question the validity of the prevalent notion that sharp enmities divided Ottoman society into various social and religious groups. There is a commonly held opinion that the Bektashis were seen as different from, or alien to, the Ottoman state and the Sunnite majority of the state.[46] However, it seems that we have to reconsider the common notion that Bektashis were suppressed and discriminated against by some other groups in society, or we have to change the common understanding that Yunus Emre was a Bektashi, as suggested in *Vilayetname* and in many of the recent critical and source materials as well.

Commentaries

Sharh, the word for commentary in Turkish, means "explaining and interpreting difficult points, expressions, and subtleties which require careful attention."[47] The interpretation of poetry developed during the Ottoman period as a continuation of interpretation of religious texts, i.e. the Qur'an and Hadith. Later, books in other fields were interpreted for various purposes, ranging from simple rephrasing in marginalia to more complicated forms of literary interpretation in multi-volume works.

The commentaries on the poetry of Yunus Emre provide ample information about the reception of Yunus Emre in the Ottoman period. Four major commentaries[48] that I will discuss are the commentary of Şeyhzade (d.1544), the commentary of Niyazi Mısri (1618–1694), the commentary of İsmail Hakkı Bursevi (1653–1725), and the commentary of Ali Nakşibendi (18th century?).[49]

I will analyze these commentaries by asking five questions which will enable one to better distinguish the nature of the understanding of Yunus Emre's poetry in these commentaries. These questions are: how did the authors of the commentaries regard the poet—Yunus Emre, how did they view the text—the poetry of Yunus Emre, how did they view their readers, in other words for whom were their commentaries written, and finally how did they view themselves and the world. The answers to these questions will provide us with significant insight into the nature of the commentaries, Yunus Emre's intended audience, and how Ottoman intellectuals and Sufis viewed Yunus Emre.

First of all, the authors of the commentaries consider Yunus Emre to be a *wali* (saint, pl. *awliya*) with extraordinary qualities. They call him *Hazrat* Yunus,[50] an honorific title which literally means Great Presence, Sheikh Yunus *qaddasa sirruhu*,(meaning, may God sanctify him) and *qaddasa'llahu sirrahu* (as above);[51] they also apply expressions of respect that are traditionally used for Muslim saints, such as a beloved of God,[52] someone through whom God speaks,[53] and someone who knows the truth of Divinity and represents this reality in his everyday life acts and manners (*hal dili*).[54]

The authors of the commentaries consider the text, the poetry of Yunus Emre, as divinely inspired and look for wisdom behind every word and aspect of the poems. Although the poems that they discuss often had varying numbers of couplets in different manuscripts, one commentator in the sixteenth century, Şeyhzade, finds the fact that the specific poem he is interpreting has seven couplets to be of special significance, and states that it must have been intentionally composed this way. He explains the meaning of the number seven over many pages, discussing the seven heavens, the seven planets, the seven seas, the seven continents, the seven minerals, the seven days of the week, and so on.[55] Although some commentators offer alternative explanations and are well aware of the fact that the poem has various versions, they still consider the text to be divinely inspired because of the spiritual position that Yunus Emre had attained.[56]

When it comes to readers of the commentaries, they were viewed by the authors of the commentaries as people who were sympathetic to the interpretations and who were willing and ready to believe them. It is impossible to find an example where the reader is seen as someone who is critical of what they are reading or someone who needs to be convinced. The authors address them as *aziz karındaşlar*[57] (dear brothers), *ey benüm canım*[58] (o my soul), *aşık u sadık olan aziz karındaşlar ve arifler*[59] (o dear brothers and sages who are in love and loyal), and *salik karındaş*[60] (disciple brother). The informality and directness of the style can be observed in the narratives of the commentaries as well. The authors of the commentaries start addressing the reader in the middle of the interpretation, using the second person pronoun.[61] At these moments, the commentary becomes a medium for imparting certain values that are believed to be Yunus Emre's aim in the poem.

The language used in these commentaries, which can be called high Ottoman Turkish, is also a good indicator of the intended audience. The authors extensively use Arabic and Persian words and phrases. The verses of the Qur'an and hadiths are also commonly used without providing explanations in Turkish.[62] The language in these works sometimes come close to the language used in *Tacü't-Tevarih,*[63] which is a history book from the 16th century, considered to be the prime example of high-style Ottoman prose. Only one commentator uses a proverb that might be considered within the realm of folk literature both with its language and style. The proverb is *Bekle gönül tarlasın su sığırı girmesin* (Protect the field of the heart; don't let water buffalo enter [it]).[64]

It is no surprise that writing a commentary implies that the author has more to say than other people about the poem in question, as well as suggesting that he knows how to interpret the poem better than other people. This is especially true for the commentaries in question. The authors suggest, or sometimes openly express, that they had been chosen for this task. The author of the Şeyhzade commentary openly states:

> The Lord God opened the universe of existence and showed it [the interpretation of the poem] to me, after I watched and saw, all of a sudden, a seven couplet, obscure *gazel* [ghazal] of Yunus Emre caught my attention. God then showed me, one by one, the subtler meaning of this seven-couplet *gazel*.[65]

In the commentary of Niyazi Mısri, Mısri explains that he wrote the commentary and then waited for a while. One night, he says, he saw Yunus Emre and Yunus Emre instructed him to change the interpretation of a particular couplet, and he did so.[66] The language used here, and especially the phrase: "let them benefit from what you wrote" uttered by Yunus Emre demonstrates the authors' perspective of their readers and how they viewed the commentary. Niyazi Mısri states:

> This helpless poor man [referring to himself in a modest way] was encouraged by some brothers to interpret a nine-couplet poem of Yunus Emre. The interpretation was left unfinished for about eight months among papers. The reason for this was that [I was wonder-

> ing] whether or not it was appropriate to the intention of the Saint [Yunus Emre]. One night, I saw Yunus Emre.[67] He showed great reception and favor and said: "Don't withhold from the poor and seekers the commentary and the fine meaning that you wrote for my words." He warned me "to give it to them and let them benefit from it." And he told this poor one "don't write what you have written for the meaning of the couplet of *İplik verdim çulhaya*." He said: "Write this meaning!" and told me what I was supposed to write. I had written a different interpretation for this couplet. I removed that one and this [new] interpretation was written.[68]

The names quoted and referred to in the commentaries presume the reader's knowledge of the great names in the history of Sufi thought. In the commentaries, the names Ibn Arabi,[69] Rumi,[70] Hallaj,[71] Fakhruddin Razi,[72] Zaynal Abidin,[73] and Junayd al-Baghdadi[74] are mentioned in a way that suggests the reader knows them and accepts their authority. The commentators use couplets[75] from Rumi's *Mathnawi* to explain certain points in the poetry of Yunus Emre, and examples from Ibn Arabi are introduced and discussed.[76]

In light of the information outlined above, it would be safe to draw the following conclusions: The authors of the commentaries did not consider Yunus Emre to be primarily a poet. Nowhere in these commentaries is he referred to as a poet, nor is there any mention of the aesthetic value of his poems. Although the commentators use poetic terms like *ghazal* and couplet, they view these poems above all as expressions of specific experiences that Yunus Emre had in his lifetime, and as explanations of the Sufi understanding of human existence. This should not, in any way be taken to mean that Sufis did not appreciate literary works or did not produce aesthetically well-developed works of art. The case is absolutely the opposite. Within Islamic civilization, intense aesthetic endeavors took place in or around Sufi circles, whether in the form of calligraphy, poetry, or architecture. However, the commentators view the poetry of Yunus Emre as a reflection of Divine wisdom. Without forgetting the aesthetic quality of Sufi poetry, we have to make a distinction between

Sufi and other types of poetry, such as Divan poetry. It is true that the lines between Divan and Sufi poetry are sometimes blurred and in some cases, such as with the works of Sheikh Galip (1702–1795), it is impossible to identify the borders between the two poetic traditions.[77] However, the fundamental differences between these two types of poetry force us to make this distinction.

Commentaries view Sufi poetry as a realm in which reality is expressed. Moreover, the fact that the great majority of people shared the Sufis' basic view of reality can be seen in these commentaries.

Sufis have a teleological understanding of the universe. We observe reflections of this understanding both in the poetry of Yunus Emre and the commentaries. The commentators find wisdom behind every word, expression, and feature in Yunus Emre's poems in the same way that they seek and see a Divine purpose behind every divine act in the universe.

The style and language used in the commentaries demonstrate that the well-educated elite appreciated the poetry of Yunus Emre. Contrary to what has been said about the readership of Yunus Emre, these commentaries are evidence of his popularity among the so-called upper classes of Ottoman society.

In the commentaries, there is no reference to whether or not Yunus Emre used Turkish, Persian, or Arabic in his poems. As far as the origin of the words used in the commentaries, there is a strong parallel between the poetry of Yunus Emre and the commentaries. In other words, almost half of the words are Arabic and Persian in origin. This shows that Yunus Emre was well appreciated not only by the unlettered masses, as apparent in the legends of oral tradition, but also among the Persian and Arabic reading elites.

Although there are different interpretations of the same poems in the commentaries, it is easy to find a common ground, which can be called Islamic mysticism; this is particularly evident in the works of Ibn Arabi and Qushayri. Commentators refer to the works of Ibn Arabi either with or without mentioning his name. Another significant issue in relation to the commentaries is that it is very difficult to see a fragmentation among the *tariqa*s, although this has been asserted by some 20th century scholars, such as Gölpınarlı.[78] Even the simple fact that members of various *tariqa*s wrote commentaries dealing with the works of Yunus Emre demonstrates that there was a form of peaceful interaction and acceptance of each other among various brotherhoods. A Nakhshi commentator has referred to Zaynal Abidin by quoting from *Ihya al-Ulumi'd Din*,[79] while other commentators have referred to Rumi or Ibn Arabi to explain the poems of Yunus Emre, who 20th century scholars have claimed to be a Bektashi, Qalandari, or Mevlevi.

Music

The poetry of Yunus Emre has always been appreciated and held in great respect among the members of various mystical orders, and his poems have been set to music in many different musical arrangements. His poems were set to music and sung not only by the ordinary people, but also at court and among the Ottoman elite. Although there are some important drawbacks that prevent us from thoroughly tracing the reception of Yunus Emre among composers during the Ottoman period, the available information on this issue clearly demonstrates that the poetry of Yunus Emre was often set to music.

The first major drawback is the fact that the musical works were not commonly written down. The transmission of this tradition was mostly oral.[80] Musical compositions were passed down from generation to generation, from master to apprentice, not only in Sufi circles, but also in many other traditions, such as *aşık*[81] poetry. With the abolishment of the Sufi brotherhoods in Turkey in 1925, this tradition came to an abrupt end. Although there were some efforts to maintain the age-old richness and refinement of these traditions, the remnants we have today must be considered minimal.

For example, Rauf Yekta, a Turkish musicologist and Mevlevi dervish during the 1920s, provided an account of an incident from the early 18th century. According to his account, the appointment of a certain Kamber Hafiz as the *serzakir* (head of the *dhikr* circle) "was the cause of scandal due to the fact that Kamber had a repertoire of 'only' three thousand pieces!"[82] The account of the great Turkish composer, poet, and calligrapher, Buhurizade Mustafa Efendi, commonly known as Itri[83] (1640? –1712?), is also very similar to this. Yahya Kemal suggests that Itri composed more than one thousand works, but only twenty of them are now available.[84] This account does not seem to be an exaggeration, since our documented information on Yunus Emre also confirms such a wealth of compositions.[85] There are documents which show that the poetry of Yunus Emre was set to music and sung both by the upper class and other classes in society. In a collection in the Süleymaniye Library in Istanbul there are thirty-three *ilahi*s (dervish hymns) by Yunus Emre that are to be sung in various *maqam*s (musical styles). Among the composers we see the names of the great masters of Ottoman court music, such as Tosunzade (d.1715), Çalakzade Şeyh Mustafa Efendi (d.1718), and Hammami İsmail Dede Efendi (d.1845).[86]

There is an illuminating article by Cemaleddin Server Revnakoğlu, which could be considered to be a testimony to the popularity of Yunus Emre among the various classes in Turkey at the turn of the 20th century.[87] Revnakoğlu gives his account of how and where the hymns of Yunus Ere were sung. In his article, he gives the specific details of the performance of Yunus Emre's poetry. According to Revnakoğlu, there was a well-established tradition of singing the poems of Yunus Emre. The poems were sung by specific groups, such as beggars, actors, water carriers and wandering dervishes. Also, they were sung at specific times, such as during the months of Ramadan and Muharram, after the *tarawih* prayer, at the congregational prayer at night during the month of Ramadan, after the Laylat al- Qadir (Night of Power), on nights in the first and second half of Ramadan, and on the seventh, fourteenth and fifteenth night following the death of a member or master of a Sufi brotherhood. These poems could also be sung on specific occasions, such as at the beginning of the *dhikr* (remembrance) ceremony, while standing or sitting down during the *dhikr*, at the end of the *dhikr*, during the first interval, when chanting became faster or more ecstatic, as well as during funeral or marriage ceremonies and when a child started going to school.

These poems were set to music in various *maqams*, and this required an extensive knowledge of music. Revnakoglu provides us with examples of the names of forty different *maqams* in which the poems of Yunus Emre were sung. Sometimes, a particular poem was set to music using more than one *maqam*. In fact, Gölpınarlı asserts that some of the poems were set to music in more than one hundred different *maqams*, and some singers and *dhakirs* (the person leading the remembrance ceremony), were praised as "the one who knows forty *şuride*," or, referring to the well-known line of a poem by Yunus Emre, as "*şuride ve şeyda kılan yarin cemalidir beni*" (What makes me confused and mad is the beauty of the beloved).[88]

Walter Feldman, a musicologist and scholar of Turkish literature, provides an example to demonstrate that the poems of Yunus Emre were sung both in orthodox and in so-called heterodox orders.[89] He discusses the various aspects of *ilahi*, and suggests that the same poems of Yunus Emre are called *ilahi* in one brotherhood, and *nefes* in another. He further asserts that *ilahi*s used in *dhikr* ceremonies were used not because of their literary value, but because of who the author of the text was. He argues that only the *ilahi*s written by the *khalifa*s, or the masters of that specific brotherhood, are used in *dhikr* ceremonies. He also argues that the reason for this was for instructive purposes. The only exception to this rule was Yunus Emre's poetry. Revnakoğlu also confirms this tradition. This further demonstrates that Yunus Emre was beyond all brotherhoods and groups, not in the sense that he was different from them, but in the sense that all Sufis found something that appealed to them in his poetry.

It is likely that Yunus Emre also sang his poems. There are interpretations that a number of them were sung by *ashiks*[90] accompanied by *saz* (a long necked lute) or *mazhar* (a kind of tambourine).[91]

However, there is no way to verify this. The only textual evidence available is a 15th century book that states that the teacher of Yunus Emre, Tapduk Emre, played the *sheshta*, a six-stringed lute.[92]

Reception of Yunus Emre in the Modern Period (1918–today)

The interpretation of the poetry and life of Yunus Emre in the 20th century can be viewed under four categories. These are nationalist school of interpretation, the heterodox school of interpretation, the humanist school of interpretation and finally additional interpretations not considered as a school of interpretation, but which need to be addressed.

The Nationalist Mode of Interpretation

Towards the end of the Ottoman Empire, especially in the political domain, there were three major ideologies: Turkism, Islamism, and Westernism. Turkism highlighted the Turkishness of the people, both within the empire and outside, and proposed this as the ideal model. According to this model, being a Turk was and should be the cement of society. Ziya Gökalp (1875–1924) is considered the father and the major figure of this ideology.[93] In the second model, Islamism, being a Muslim was of central importance. Mehmet Akif (1873–1936), the author of the Turkish national anthem, particularly expressed this idea in his poems, and proposed a model that is exemplified by the era of Prophet Muhammad, peace and blessings be upon him.[94] He proposed taking the sciences of the West while continuing to follow the cultural and moral roots and values of Turkish society. In the third model, Westernism, the West was taken to be the perfect model in every aspect of life. Tevfik Fikret (1867–1915), who refuted the whole of Ottoman history in his *Tarih-i Kadim* (Ancient History), is considered to be the leading figure of this ideology.[95] While these discussions continued in the political arena, each model produced its versions of history or highlighted specific issues in current events.

Turkish nationalism was historically late compared to the other ideologies in the empire, as it implied the end of the multi-ethnic state, at least for the Ottomans. The nationalist movements in the Ottoman Empire started with the non-Turkish groups, such as Greeks, Albanians, and Serbs. However, the late occurrence of Turkish nationalism was not related to its place on the political scene. That is to say, although it came late to the political scene, it occupied an important place in the following years in Turkish society. Eventually Turkish nationalism and Westernism became the dominant ideologies for the Republic of Turkey.

The history of Turkish nationalism starts with history books, dictionaries, literary activities, and the activities of outsiders, such as the intellectuals coming from Russia and Central Asia, or scholars who were studying Turkish history and culture outside of Turkey. As mentioned already, the main figure in theorizing this ideology was Ziya Gökalp, the author of *Türkçülüğün Esasları* (The Principles of Turkism).[96] However, there is another prominent intellectual who played a more important role in presenting Turkish nationalism in a more concrete and scholarly way, Fuat Köprülü (1894–1962). Fuat Köprülü is accepted as the founder of Turkish literary studies. He is also recognized as the first person to write extensive scholarly works on Yunus Emre. The first of these works was *Türk Edebiyatında İlk Mutasavvıflar* (The First Mystics in Turkish Literature), which demonstrates his great capacity as a scholar. Köprülü used sources in Arabic, Persian, French and German, and was familiar with modern historiography and relevant historical and modern sources. However, the same book also indicates the paradigm from which he was writing. Köprülü was writing at a time when intellectuals were looking for a solution to the future of the empire, and in this process he proposed nationalism as the perfect model. The other works of Fuat Köprülü and his political activities reveal his commitment to this goal.[97]

The main thesis of *Türk Edebiyatında İlk Mutasavvıflar* (The First Mystics in Turkish Literature) is that Western Turkish literature, i.e. Ottoman literature, is the continuation of the Turkish/Turkic literatures from other areas, especially in Central Asia, and it is particularly in mystical folk literature that one can observe this continuity. The main framework that Köprülü bases his thesis on is that all Turkish/Turkic literatures should be considered as a whole. The book was considered both by the author and by many intellectuals of the time to be revolutionary. When we look at the details of the book critically, we see that the only different idea or method in this book is extending nationalism from the political arena to literary historiography, and considering Turkish literature as a whole, as a distinct entity that is separate from multicultural, multilingual, and multiethnic Muslim Eastern literatures; this eventually created the idea that Turkish literature is the literature written in Turkish by Turks.

Having emphasized the necessity and vitality of a theory that in particular would shape the literary history and in general the humanities/social sciences, Köprülü made explicit his theory. The theory in the book is that "various Turkish/Turkic groups are not independent from one another and therefore they should not be counted as different *millet* (nations)." Köprülü uses the word *millet* here, which has various equivalents in Turkish. For the Ottoman state, the word *millet* denotes the religious and ethnic groups of the state, as in the *millet* system, while in Islamist ideology it refers to the Muslim community (*ummah*) and in Turkism, as alluded to by Köprülü, it means members of the same nation. In this distinction, the determining factors are language and race (*ırk*). However the champions of Turkism are very careful to distinguish themselves from a purely racist ideology. It was for this and some other practical reasons that another Turkish nationalist, Ziya Gökalp, a predecessor of Köprülü, made a specific definition for the term race. He explicitly stated that anyone who feels themselves to be a Turk should be considered a Turk.[98]

Another major element in Köprülü's book and theory is his motive for writing about the matter in the first place. He explains that his concern was "to find a period in the literary history of the Turks that could be considered to reflect a national spirit and national aesthetic sensibility."[99] For this purpose, he chose Ahmed Yesevi (ca. 1102–1166/7) and Yunus Emre. For Köprülü, these two poets, especially Yunus Emre, had produced works that exemplified his concept of a national spirit and aesthetic sensibility. Köprülü evaluates these two poets and their followers within the context of mystical folk literature. For Köprülü, the characteristics of mystical folk literature are derived from general folk literature, Islam, and neo-Platonism. The language, style, and meter are based on folk literature, while the mystical and moral elements are from Islam and neo-Platonism. As one of the reasons why he choose this period and this literature, Köprülü explains: "Since our own national identity was forgotten under the Persian influence in the past and since the *Tanzimat* was under the influence of the West, as with everything that belongs to the people, this mystical folk literature too has been considered contemptible."[100] For Köprülü, what is important in this literature is its relation to the national identity.

In this classification, it is difficult not to see a remarkable similarity to the views of the Orientalist E. J. W. Gibb,[101] who expressed the idea "that great race [i.e. Turks]… has never produced any religion, philosophy or literature which bears the stamp of its individual genius"[102] and they have been "unable to originate any literature which should give expression to the true genius of their race."[103]

Gibb discusses the information provided by biographers, such as Aşık Çelebi and Taşköprülüzade. The issues discussed by Gibb are: Yunus Emre's illiteracy, his spiritual teacher Tapduk Emre, his carrying wood from the forest for 40 years, the time period in which he is believed to have lived, and the features of his poems. Then Gibb analyzes the matters of the poems in a short but comprehensive way. He considers the poems to be transcendental and for Gibb, Yunus is the first Turkish poet who did not have a model. He also points out the similarities between Rumi, the great Sufi of the 13th century, and Yunus, saying, "all the philosophy of Yunus will be found in the Divan of Jelal."[104]

One important thing that Gibb comments on is the issue of how literary biographers consider Yunus Emre. On this issue, Gibb presents a point of view, which no matter how unsubstantiated, is repeated again and again by many later writers. It is also used by both Turkish and non-Turkish scholars.[105] Gibb cites the biographers who assert that Yunus could barely read and he arrives at this conclusion: "The mere fact that his verses are in the native and not the Persian meters is itself enough to stamp him a barbarian in the eyes of these literary mandarins; it was enough to make Latifi and Hasan Çelebi exclude him altogether from their memoirs."[106]

There are some factual and conceptual problems with this statement. It is true that the two biographers cited did not mention Yunus Emre. However, others, such as Aşık Çelebi, Taşköprülüzade, and Hoca Saadettin—the author of *Tacü't-Tevarih*, the history book accepted to be the most artistic example of Ottoman prose[107]—mention his name. It is also true that these authors claim that Yunus Emre was illiterate. However, they do this not to denigrate Yunus Emre, or as Gibb put it, "to stamp him as a barbarian," but to elevate him. As Gibb quotes from Aşık Çelebi, "Yunus was of the number of those perfect ones who are pulled by the hook of the Divine attraction from the world of the Kingdom to the world of the Angelry."[108] "He was of the saintly guests who translated the language of the lips into the language of the heart, and of those Companions of the Secret who spoke with the voice of the Unseen World."[109] In these lines, one can see that being illiterate is not in any way a negative feature. It indicates that the biographers believe in the Divine inspiration of the poetry of Yunus Emre.

It is quite possible that Gibb adapted what some of the Ottoman intellectuals, such as Ziya Paşa, thought about the folk-elite division. Ziya Paşa (1825–1880), as part of a movement which praised everything considered "folk" and denigrated everything considered "Ottoman," or "Divan," expressed very similar ideas in the last half of the 19th century. Later, finding these views extreme, Ziya Paşa changed his outlook quite drastically.[110] Both sources, those used by Gibb and the ones discussed above in the "Reception of Yunus Emre in the Ottoman Period," demonstrate the unsubstantiated nature of Gibb's assertion that Ottoman biographers considered Yunus Emre to be a barbarian, and indeed this statement is contrary to historical and textual evidence.[111]

The commonality between Köprülü and Gibb is that both consider Yunus Emre to be separate from the elites of Ottoman society, although both of them provide examples showing that this was not the case. The difference between Gibb and Köprülü is that Gibb believes and explicitly states that the Turks could not create any products of civilization that bore its own stamp, whereas Köprülü asserts just the opposite and writes the monograph on Yunus Emre to prove his thesis.

When we consider the theoretical framework of Köprülü, we can say that it is an adaptation of Ziya Gökalp's nationalism to literary historiography. Thirty years before Köprülü wrote this book, Gökalp had expressed the same ideas using almost the same sentences in asserting that the Turkish people in the Ottoman Empire had been denigrated. As demonstrated later by Ahmet Hamdi Tanpınar, Gökalp's ideas were disorganized, lacked a coherent structure, and were based on marginal examples, misinterpretations, and sometimes even intentional or unintentional misreadings.[112] Both Gökalp and Köprülü argued that Turkishness was not represented fairly in many domains of Ottoman culture, such as within the mainstream literature. For this reason, both men looked for cultural productions in which Turkishness is reflected, offering different examples for this. Gökalp argued the superiority of pre-Islamic Turkish culture, and tried to create a counter culture around pre-Islamic military heroes, such as Attila and Chengiz Khan, to make them society's new "role models." Köprülü offers mystical folk literature as an example of a literary genre that exemplifies a national identity.

The most important issue in Köprülü's presentation is his ideological stance, which compels him to look for a pure and original product that reflects Turkish national aesthetic sensibility.[113] Not only in *Türk Edebiyatında İlk Mutasavvıflar* (The First Mystics in Turkish Literature), but also in other works, for example in his five-volume *Türk Saz Şairleri* (Turkish Saz Poets), he makes this point very clear. In his *Türk Saz Şairleri* (Turkish Saz Poets), Köprülü explicitly warns the reader not to think that *ashik* literature reflects the aesthetic sensibility of Turks. In Köprülü's view, *ashik* literature had degenerated since it used some elements from the literature of the elite and thus had lost its purity.

The second important issue in *Türk Edebiyatında İlk Mutasavvıflar* (The First Mystics in Turkish Literature) is Köprülü's assertion that there were various social classes in the Ottoman Empire and these classes felt a mutual antagonism. Earlier, Gökalp argued the same idea by highlighting the expression of "*etrak-ı bi-idrak*" (uncomprehending Turks), a term supposedly used by the Ottoman elite for the Turkish speaking lower classes. Köprülü repeats the same idea by saying that "the poets who slavishly copied Persian poets, seeing the fact that Yunus Emre's poems were read with a great joy among the people, wanted to take revenge either by considering them outside the realm of poetry or by belittling them."[114] Like Gökalp, Köprülü also believed that the pre-Islamic past of the Turks was original and authentic. He states, "actually there was a primitive originality in all the social institutions, in the language, religion, morality, customs and law of that time."[115] Elsewhere he asserts that "this primitive but lively and sincere literature developed on the Asian steppes with a majesty and power that was rich enough to reflect the harsh and warrior-like, but at the same time, delicate and deep spirit of Turks."[116]

It is easy to understand the perspective of Fuat Köprülü if we analyze his political and ideological stance and what he wanted to achieve politically. Köprülü was a Turkish nationalist and strongly believed that the future of Ottoman/Turkish society was dependent upon nationalism. To realize this purpose, certain changes had to be carried out. One of the things needed was the creation of a past for nationalism that would give a sense of continuity, a sense of eternity, with the past and the future. Gökalp tried to do this by referring to the pre-Islamic past. However, there was a six-century-gap between 19th century nationalism and its imagined, created past. There was nothing to show continuity over six centuries. Moreover, the products of the pre-Islamic past were very limited. Some intellectuals, including the famous minister of education, Hasan Ali Yücel, (1897–1961) and at one point, Yahya Kemal (1884–1958),[117] tried another source; they looked to the ancient civilizations in Anatolia as the basis for modern Turkish society, and took this to "an extreme and laughable point" as Benedict Anderson puts it in his *Imagined Communities*.[118] It might seem unimportant and inconceivable from today's point of view, however, looking for a different past and trying very hard to establish this was a serious state policy and found a good deal of support from some of the intellectuals of the time. More importantly, it had a very important impact on disconnecting the ties of Turkish society with the Ottoman past.

According to this idea, the cultural source for modern Turkish society was and should be the ancient Anatolian civilizations, such as the Hittites and Sumerians. The names of many state banks, such as Sümerbank and Etibank, the logos of major universities in Turkey, such as Ankara University and Hacettepe University, many public statues in Turkish cities, as well as the fact that there is not a single item from the Seljukid or Ottoman period in the Museum of Anatolian Civilizations in the capital city, Ankara, are some examples of this concept at work.[119]

Fuat Köprülü selected a past for Turkish society which was supposed to show its true nature even at a time when it was suppressed. Unlike Gökalp, he chose a segment of Turkish/Ottoman society, instead of a dead past. In his view, mystical folk literature, specifically the poetry of Yunus Emre, connected Turkish society to Central Asia, and from there to its pre-Islamic past. Thus, for Köprülü, Yunus Emre was the channel of a national past. What Köprülü does is to imagine a community which had not been imagined before. As he indicated in *Türk Edebiyatında İlk Mutasavvıflar* (The First Mystics in Turkish Literature), nobody previously had conceived of various Turkish/Turkic groups as a united community. He uses the work of Yunus Emre as a case to prove his thesis. However, his political attachment and his motivation prevented him from seeing the obvious commonalities between Yunus Emre and other figures who lived in the same geography around the same time period, such as Rumi and Fakhruddin Iraqi.

The Heterodox Mode of Interpretation

One of the recent schools of interpretation of Yunus Emre asserts that he was an Alevite-Bektashi poet who reflected this in his poetry.[120] One has to carefully note that this Alevite-Bektashi understanding is very different from, and sometimes contrary to, that of the one outlined in the main reference works of the *Bektashiyya*, such as the *Vilayetname* of Hacı Bektaş Veli or the works of major scholars in this field, such as Irene Melikoff or Ahmet Yaşar Ocak.[121] According to this mode of interpretation, Yunus Emre is portrayed as the representative of the periphery as opposed to the center, as the representative of the people as opposed to the elite, as the representative of heterodoxy as opposed to orthodoxy. He is also portrayed as the representative of the pre-Islamic past and values of the Turks as opposed to later developments, such as the conversion to Islam; he is even represented as the representative of Indian, Zoroastrian, Christian or New Platonic ideas, as opposed to cultural developments in Muslim societies, including the Seljukid society. No matter how simplistic and radical these dichotomies seem, they are asserted and reiterated again and again in this mode of interpretation.

Instead of discussing these elements one by one, I will discuss them within a broader context that is derived from this interpretation and covers all the elements; namely, anti-Seljukism, or anti-Ottomanism, and anti-Islamism. These two concepts build the main framework of this mode of interpretation. This interpretation asserts that Yunus Emre was an Alevite-Bektashi dervish and that this is obvious in his poetry.[122] In his poetry, it continues, there is a deep love for Ali. This interpretation defines Yunus Emre for what he is not rather than for what he is. It is argued that Yunus Emre was a Sufi; however this idea of Sufism is not something that originated from Islam or is even heavily influenced by it. Islam is considered to be just a small part of one of the three major elements that formed Sufism. These three elements are the influence of civilizations that existed in Anatolia prior to Islam; the remnants of ancient Asian religions, such as Zoroastrianism, which came to Anatolia with the migrating Turks and the interactions of the Islamized people in Anatolia with the other groups, such as Christians in Anatolia.[123] Sometimes, even this minimal influence of Islam is omitted and Sufism is presented as a "different version of New Platonism,"[124] or even "a different version of polytheism."[125] After making a strong connection between polytheism and Sufism, or New Platonism and Sufism, the authors give examples highlighting the so-called obvious contradictions between Islam and the poetry of Yunus Emre. According to this interpretation, there is always a contradiction in Yunus Emre's poetry because "sometimes he is tied to Islam and sometimes to mysticism."[126] This so-called contradiction is explained by the champions of this interpretation as the product of the two periods in his life. In the first period Yunus Emre is respectful to Islam, and in the second period he rebels against God and becomes a completely different person. Since there is no historical or textual evidence to support this periodization, it is easy to understand that the authors are merely constructing a story to support their argument. Indeed they cannot agree: There are two different versions of this periodization. In the first version, when

Yunus Emre was young, "he was a fearless, careless poet against Sharia; in his elderly years, he devoted himself to prayer, and became a 'Muslim' who begs forgiveness for what he did."[127] In the second version, this periodization is just the opposite. Yunus Emre was a so-called pro-Sharia poet and later he became a traveler on the Sufi path.[128] Needless to say that in this interpretation it is argued that he composed poems that suggest some religious sentiments in both periods. In order to make the asserted dichotomy between Islam and Sufism the authors either do not mention the obvious Islamic origin of certain concepts or mention it vaguely and dismissively. When love and affection is discussed, İsmet Zeki Eyüboğlu states, "if this word [i.e. love] is understood in the sense of 'unifying, harmonizing, its root is from the First Age and its creator is Empedocles."[129] However, when he mentions a well-known hadith qudsi on the same issue, he says, "according to an ancient Islamic belief, God wanted to be known because of the love that He had for himself."[130] In the writings of the authors who favor this mode of interpretation, it is asserted that what Yunus Emre suggests is against Islam and "the products of a perception that violates all the conditions of the religion of Islam."[131] Yunus Emre "under the cover of Sufism … frees himself from all the restrictions that religion imposes."[132] Eyüboğlu goes one step further and takes Yunus Emre beyond all monotheistic religions: "This is the perspective of three religions. However, Sufism [has] a completely different [perspective]."[133] After discussing a poem, Eyüboğlu concludes: "It is worth reconsidering, to question the connection of a poet who speaks this way to the religion of Islam."[134]

Authors, such as Başgöz and Eyüboğlu, also apply their criticism and accusations to other issues, judging the entire Muslim history and culture. İsmet Zeki Eyüboğlu discusses the term "universality" vaguely and comes to the following conclusion: "Islam asserts universality. However, in its 1400 years of application, there has been no example [of this]. How can a religion become universal, a religion that does not give right to life for those who do not think like itself, a religion that asserts that only through itself the right, the good and the beautiful can be known? The same thing holds true for Christianity too. We can say that today the religion of Islam does not have any universality at all."[135]

In his work, *Yunus Emre*, İlhan Başgöz tries to explain the origin of Sufism; his criticism extends to the whole of Middle Eastern societies and history. Başgöz cites an article that explains the source of Christian mysticism. According to the argument presented in the article, the sexual energy of monastic Christians was not spent, and from this unspent sexual energy arose mystic love. However, for Başgöz, the fact that there is no monastic life in Muslim societies poses a threat to this valid (in his view) explanation. On the basis of this article Başgöz offers the following unsubstantiated, accusatory, and ahistorical account of why mysticism emerged in Muslim societies:

> […] but there is another characteristic in Middle Eastern societies that helps facilitate the sublimation of love and detach it from the human body. In this region, where even religion is accommodated according to the desires of men, women are considered devils, liars, deceivers, untrustworthy, and lowly creatures. Hating women is a very common tradition in these societies. Heeding the word of women brings disaster. One of the Muslim Sufis says, "I am not afraid of any creature as much as I am afraid of women." Look at the lack of value given to women: The son of the fourth caliph, Hasan, married 250 women! His father had married only ten women… In these kinds of societies, whether Muslim or Christian, real love and desire for women cannot bloom. The huge gap within man created by this is easily filled with abstract love.[136]

Other than many false assumptions, such as the possibility that Hasan had 250 wives, it is not difficult to observe in these lines the essentializing Orientalist perspective that sweeps the entire history of the region under one explanation, as well as the psychoanalytical theory, that is, the idea that sexuality or sexual desire is the main impetus of every activity in life. Certainly, there have been problems regarding women in Middle Eastern societies, just as there have been in many other societies. One cannot, however, deny that Ottoman women also enjoyed many progressive rights in this region that were unavailable to women in European countries, such as the right of married Ottoman women to own real estate and other property, unlike European women at the same period.[137] It is also interesting to note that one of the main goals of Sufism, training the ego, something that is not easy to do in any way, is shown by Başgöz to be an automatic, natural outcome of a very common characteristic of Middle Eastern societies. Sufism, which has many aspects and certainly played very important roles in the life of individuals and societies, cannot be reduced to the level of a regional development that was achieved without effort. Although the author seems very careful about establishing his arguments on historical sources, he does not provide any sources for the information that he cites for the case of Ali, the father of Hasan.

In the heterodox school of interpretation, authors, aware of the fact that their theory of a young, rebellious Yunus versus the old dervish, or a young mullah versus the old dervish, has no textual or historical basis, attempt to explain the religious content and tone of Yunus Emre's poetry by calling him "a poet of contradictions."[138] Another explanation is that "he did not have the options to think differently… it is difficult to divert from the path that the age imposes"[139] and "if he had lived today, he would struggle against the things that the most modern poet is struggling against." Eyüboğlu even suggests that,

> Yunus Emre fell in love with a beauty who was near him and made all of his poems look as if they were addressed to God in order to save himself from religious oppression,"[140]

an idea that is also found in Gölpınarlı.[141]

The second major element that has formed this mode of interpretation is an anti-Seljukid and anti-Ottoman attitude. One can easily argue that in this mode of interpretation of Yunus Emre, there is not a single positive reference to the Seljukid or Ottoman states. The Seljukids and Ottomans were considered to represent orthodoxy, central control, the establishment, and were seen as colonizers and oppressors. However almost every other non-Ottoman or non-Seljukid element that existed around this period and in this geography is mentioned and given credit for creating the poetry of Yunus Emre.

When the relationship between the state and the people is discussed, Eyüboğlu says,

> There is no connection between the people of rural areas and the well-to do minority. [We see] all the signs of making rural areas, which were productive, the center of exploitation. Anatolia was an environment in which two different societies lived. This separation, which was to continue for centuries, sometimes led to rebellions and massacres.[142]

The Ottoman state is presented as something that is in contradiction to Yunus Emre's values. For instance, the poetry of Yunus Emre is universal, however:

> The Ottoman understanding was not universal. Even its local attitude was based on interest. The Ottoman government did not fight against the poor societies to spread the religion of Islam. The ideology of the Ottoman government was to take over the territories of wealthy nations. To make a long story short, the Ottoman government was the center of exploitation.[143]

The internal logic of this argument poses a contradiction. On the one hand, the Seljukid and Ottoman government are portrayed as religious, orthodox entities. On the other hand, it is suggested that they made a distinction between the rich regions and the poor regions. The anti-Seljukid and anti-Ottoman attitude in this interpretation becomes more obvious when we compare how other elements in the same period are treated.

İsmet Zeki Eyüboğlu argues that

> [...] we must not overlook the Christian medieval ages of Anatolia; more importantly, we cannot say it is *bizden değildir* (not part of us) and thus eliminate it. This is against scientific

> reality. To be proud and say that the hands that made the Seljukid tiles came from the Tanrı Mountains is far from bringing scientific proof; it is a matter of ridicule.[144]

The Tanrı Mountains represent the central Asian roots of the Turkish people in Anatolia. Here Eyüboğlu is criticizing Köprülü, who considers Yunus Emre as a Turkish Sufi akin to the Central Asian Ahmet Yesevi and argues that Yunus Emre's work is a continuation of the literature and tradition that was started in Central Asia and continued in Anatolia. Denying the Turkish influence on Sufis in Anatolia, İsmet Zeki Eyüboğlu is eager to emphasize a Persian contribution: "Persian intellectuals had a prolific and developed past in terms of civilization. The thought of Persia was enriched by the civilization developed in India."[145] It is true that Persia had a developed civilization when Yunus Emre lived in Anatolia and the people in Anatolia borrowed many elements from the Persian cultural sphere, such as religious terminology and literary elements. However, what the author is doing is connecting Persian civilization to India and ultimately reducing Sufism to an Indian influence.

The names of Neo-Platonists, Egyptian pharaohs, Babylonian and Sumerian kings, Zoroastrian Persians,[146] Pericles,[147] Mateos of Urfa (d. 12th c.)[148] Plato,[149] and Aristotle[150] are all given for the explanation of the poetry of Yunus Emre and to prove the so-called connection between the cultures that these names represent and the poetry of Yunus Emre. However, there are few, if any, references to Ibn Arabi, Fakhruddin Iraqi, Sadreddin Konevi, Qurayshi or any other major intellectuals of the times; the works of these people would actually help in understanding and explaining the poetry and time of Yunus Emre. Surprisingly, the name of Rumi is mentioned as an argument that he was absolutely different from and had no connection with Yunus Emre. "Rumi, who wrote all of his poems in Persian, was not from us (*bizden değildi*) as far as ideas and beliefs are concerned."[151]

It is ironic that İsmet Zeki Eyüboğlu uses the same phrase for Rumi, "*bizden değildi*" that he used to criticize those who do not consider medieval Anatolian Christianity to be part of Sufi culture.

One can ask the hypothetical question of whether writing in a different language makes someone completely different. If so, we must note that none of the names that İsmet Zeki Eyüboğlu wants the reader to consider in relation to Yunus Emre wrote in Turkish. İsmet Zeki Eyüboğlu and İlhan Başgöz explicitly and repeatedly suggest that one should take medieval Christianity, Zoroastrianism, and New Platonic ideas into consideration, but not Rumi or the culture of Seljukid society. İsmet Zeki Eyüboğlu provides a number of suggestions for how one can better understand Yunus Emre, and the first item in this list is the following: "In order to understand and explain Yunus Emre, one has to abandon all of his thoughts that are related to religion."[152] In the seventh item of this list, Eyüboğlu makes a suggestion, which is the heart and the underlying point of his interpretation of Yunus Emre. He states:

> The language of Yunus Emre is the topic of another study. It is a unique source to determine the stages of the development of Turkish. With this language, not only is poetry written, but also some problems are analyzed, presented, and brought into the realm of discussion. The language of Yunus Emre is proof that Turkish can become a powerful language of philosophy. This philosophy does not need to be inspired by medieval theology. The concepts have the ability to comprehend certain theories. By taking these concepts away from Sufism, the possibility of enriching them with a new perspective and improving them are many. One should not avoid thinking with them. Yunus, who adopted some of these concepts into Turkish, opened a way. Without using Arabic, Turkish words, thinking in Turkish, is sufficient[153]

The phrase "taking away" (*elinden almak*) is quite revealing here. It has a negative connotation in Turkish and it conveys the meaning of taking something from someone, usually by force. The author could have used many different phrases, such as, "to use" (*kullanmak*), "to adapt" (*uyarlamak*), "to benefit from" (*yararlanmak*), or "to utilize" (*işlerlik kazandırmak*). However he uses the phrase "*elinden almak*." The word choice explains the attitude of the heterodox interpretation, which is "taking away" the poetry and personality of Yunus

Emre from its historical, social, and religious context, and using it for another purpose. Since every other argument supports this idea, this little phrase cannot be considered to be a "slip of the pen."

What I have termed the heterodox mode of interpretation, in fact, displaces Yunus Emre both culturally and socially and locates him beyond the pale in the realm of negative myth. For example, the groundless notion that Alevites have sexual relations with their family members is not taken seriously in any segment of society. Yet Başgöz, in presenting details about the brotherhood that Yunus Emre belonged to, quotes Gölpınarlı and Turan about Tapduklular, arguing that these people believed in and prayed to trees, and presented their wives, sisters and daughters to guests who came to their house. Başgöz implicitly approves the alleged information about this group and adds more examples of this type of custom, which he calls "sexual hospitality," among North African societies.[154] I. Z. Eyüboğlu, on the other hand, connects the origin of the Alevite-Bektashi brotherhoods to the Christian groups of Anatolia[155] or sometimes to polytheism[156] and characterizes them as totally opposed to and separate from Islam.[157]

It is difficult to understand the internal logic of the heterodox mode of interpretation, as it neither conforms to the historical and textual data that are currently available regarding Yunus Emre and his period, nor does it help to promote any political or religious group in modern Turkish society. The overriding element to be observed in this mode of interpretation is the notion that Yunus Emre did not have a strong Muslim component in either his poetry or his personality.

Humanist Mode of Interpretation

Along with nationalist and heterodox interpretations of the poetry and personality of Yunus Emre, a humanist interpretation can be seen in many works.[158] In this mode of interpretation, as the name suggests, Yunus Emre is considered to be a prime example, a forerunner, and indeed, a representative of humanism and his poetry is seen as one of the finest examples of this philosophy. In works adhering to this interpretation, it is difficult to find a full-fledged definition or explanation of what is understood by the term humanism. However, from bits and pieces, it can be understood that humanism means loving human beings just because they are human and giving ultimate importance to them rather than to the Divine, and not considering the human being in the context of a Divine hierarchy.

The humanist interpretations present Yunus Emre as a representative of tolerance and a fighter against dogma. He is "the first great Turkish humanist [who] stood squarely against Muslim dogmatists in expressing the primary importance of human existence and of *res humane*."[159] In addition, he "makes 'love' as the religion of humanity."[160] There is an emphasis on how the members of other cultures and religions are perceived by Yunus Emre: "His poems frequently refer to his full acceptance of the four holy books rather than a strict adherence to the Qur'an,"[161] and "his philosophy is akin to Socratic humanism."[162] Or, "he was [also] akin to Petrarch and Erasmus."[163] The names of Homer,[164] François Villan,[165] Dante, Shakespeare, and Cervantes[166] are also given as being related to Yunus Emre. In this mode of interpretation, Yunus Emre is viewed as the mouthpiece/representative of "all the people, Hittite, pagan, Christian, and Muslim, who lived in our lands."[167]

In the works of authors who assert this idea, a clear pattern of considering Sufism and Islam as two separate entities can be seen. The authors that interpret Yunus Emre as a humanist often compare the concepts of Islam and Sufism. In this comparison, "dogma claims that God, who created the earth and human beings, is outside the world and unlike His creations. But the Sufi view holds that God is inclusive to the universe and that there is no dichotomy between God and man..."[168] Günay also suggests the same dichotomy: "Yunus is far removed from a concept of a God who created the world, sent the people into it and is watching them from His skies."[169]

In the case of Halman, one motivation that might explain this mode of interpretation is his expected readership. He was writing in English and for people who generally know little about the background and intellectual sources of Yunus Emre. It is possible that he wanted to use a language that would be helpful in explaining Yunus Emre's poetry. The second possible motivation might be to overcome the view of European or American readership about Turkish, which is not very different that of from E.J.W. Gibb, who considers the Turkish "race" impotent with respect to the ability to produce any religion or philosophy.

Another motivation might be an attempt to establish a parallel between Western history and Muslim history. In this construction, the medieval ages are considered to be a dark age, regardless of East or West, and what the West produced as a reaction to this age, which is humanism, is the equivalent of Sufism. Halman states, "the Muslim zealots, like the bigots of medieval Christianity, preached submission to God, denial of the human worth, and strict observance of religious practices. Yunus Emre and other mystics denigrated these views."[170] This Western influence and perspective of issues in some of the works that advocate this interpretation can be seen not only in the case of Yunus Emre, but also in the evaluation of previous scholarship. For instance, in 1981 Sebahattin Eyüboğlu said that, "the first person who considered Yunus Emre seriously, who analyzed Yunus Emre from a Western view of poetry, was Burhan Toprak."[171] In these lines, it is easy to see how the words Western and serious are used interchangeably. However, the fact that the author does not even mention *Türk Edebiyatında İlk Mutasavvıflar* (The First Mystics in Turkish Literature) by Köprülü, which was published in 1918, is of even greater significance. Although the book does have a political perspective, it is without question a scholarly work of outstanding caliber which provides an excellent analysis of Yunus Emre and the dervish brotherhoods of the time. One thing that makes Toprak's work so appealing to certain segments of the Turkish intellectual elite is that he compares Yunus Emre to Dante Alighieri, and calls Yunus Emre's *Divan* "our Divine Commedia."[172]

One can question the validity of Toprak's comparison. Dante has very definite categories for those who are different from him. For instance, he places some of the well-known names of Islamic history in hell. However, Yunus Emre considers seventy-two nations, which is the same word for humanity, and loves them just because they were created by God, saying, "I love the created because of the Creator."

In the humanist mode of interpretation, a Marxist tone, especially in Sebahattin Eyuboğlu, can be seen. "Yunus Emre today is not the property of the *ummah*, the Islamic society, but of the nation. No matter what kind of belief, sect, or brotherhood they have, all poets should now address humanity."[173] This Marxist, socialist tone is extended to the whole of Abrahamic history: "...Moses is the rebel against the Pharaoh, Jesus is the rebel against the Romans, and Muhammad is the rebel against the Meccan notables."[174] In this mode of interpretation Yunus "supported the oppressed against the oppressor with his heart and thoughts. He is someone who elevates humanity and makes it God."[175] The concept of state versus the people is also present: "He is the Anatolian peasant whom all the states used to rob."[176] "How explicitly he could say that heaven is in the world and the reality is hidden in the soil."[177] The explanation for the existence of religions in this interpretation is simple: "Human beings created religions." "It is appropriate if a human being is called an animal which is afraid of death, because death exists only when one thinks of it. The human being has created religion, science, and art to overcome the fear of death, sometimes winning, sometimes not."[178] This explanation is meant to answer the possible question of why Yunus Emre composed so many poems that could be considered to be a clear statement paralleling the ideas introduced by Abrahamic religions.

Individual Interpretations

Some of the works on Yunus Emre in English are very important in terms of reflecting the major issues that have been discussed in

Yunus Emre scholarship in Turkey from a different perspective. In particular, one can observe the extension of larger issues about Turkish society and Islam. It is of particular importance to examine how Western scholars, or scholars who write for Western readers, present Yunus Emre.

After Gibb, the first person to write in English on Yunus Emre was J. Kingsley Birge, the author of *The Bektashi Order of Dervishes*,[179] the first serious treatment of the Bektashi order. Birge presents Yunus Emre as "a forerunner of simplification of language,"[180] "a spiritual hero… who heroically and openly struggled against evil traditions and evil doctrines."[181] As far as the biography and poetry of Yunus Emre is concerned, Birge basically repeats what was available at the time in Turkish without providing any new comments. However, there is something significant in terms of explaining the perspective and attitude of some Western scholars, both in Islam and Sufism.

Under the subtitle of "His Mohammedanism," Birge states,

> Since Yunus' nature is one of such transparent faith, his love of God so real, it is natural to ask to what extent he is indebted to Muhammad and to the formal religion of Islam for his religious experience. Several hymns attributed to Yunus in which he sings praise of Muhammad…[182]

After this questioning, Birge concludes: "Yunus is by no means a believer in the formal system of Islam."[183] These lines indicate that Birge considers Islam and Sufism to be two separate entities and in this separation, the former is viewed as non-transparent and unreal. The author thinks that it is natural to question the relationship between this type of transparent, real love and Islam, something which lacks these kinds of qualities.

The further remarks of Birge about the relationship between Islam and Sufism, or Sufism and Christianity, elaborate on this point. His comparison of the poetry of Yunus Emre to Christianity is of more significance as it is being written for a Christian readership and published in a presentation volume for an Old Testament scholar.[184] He discusses a line in which Yunus Emre says "he read four books" and dwells on the question of which translation of Bible Yunus could have read. Without reaching any definitive result, he concludes, "passages already quoted show the spirit at least of some of Jesus' teaching. The following line is strongly reminiscent of Jesus' comment to first make clean the inside of the cup that the outside may be clean also."[185]

Birge obviously does not accept Islam as a legitimate source of divine revelation or one that could naturally have some elements from the revelation that preceded it, i.e. Christianity. In this regard, he is similar to some later Turkish authors who look to Christianity, Zoroastrianism, and neo-Platonic ideas for the source of Yunus' inspiration.

The third book to discuss Yunus Emre in English is *Yunus Emre, The Wandering Fool: Sufi Poems of a 13th Century Dervish* by Edouard Roditi and Guzin Dino.[186] This book presents Yunus Emre "as a heterodox dervish ... who preserved some customs and beliefs of the Shamanistic religion... and dualistic beliefs of Persian Zoroastrianism, who was against the Seljukid establishment."[187] The authors argue that Yunus Emre was read by "the peasant and nomads who could rarely read or write, especially by members of the Kizilbash dervish brotherhood that fomented revolts against feudal tyranny, and by the village bards."

Another significant feature of the book *Yunus Emre, The Wandering Fool* is the constant effort to link Yunus Emre to other so-called "heretics" of the world. Many names are mentioned: Kaygusuz Abdal and Nesimi, 14th century heretical Turkish poets; heretical Jewish mystics; Sarmad, a 17th century heretical poet who was beheaded in India. Also, the issue of "the utterly inhuman persecution of the very peaceful followers of the Bahai faith...in contemporary Iran" is highlighted.

Roditi argues that Sufism is a reflection of pre-Islamic beliefs "such as Zoroastrianism and Manichaeism," and states, "Yunus Emre was a true ecstatic who expressed himself in riddles, which appear to be nonsensical." The authors provide no evidence for their assertion, and it is impossible to see Zoroastrian or Shamanist features in Yunus Emre's poetry. The argument that Yunus Emre was read by a group limited to peasants and nomads has also been disproved by many scholars, including Köprülü, Gölpınarlı and Feldman. Even a brief consideration of the commentaries and parallel poems composed in appreciation of Yunus Emre indicate how widespread the appreciation of his poetry was. For example, Feldman discusses the usage of poems in Sufi brotherhoods, suggesting that usually poems would be chosen from those composed by members of the same brotherhood, but Yunus' poetry was an exception. In other words, the poetry of Yunus Emre has been recited, regardless of its origin in various brotherhoods.[188] The idea that Yunus Emre expresses himself in "riddles, which appeared to be nonsensical" is also groundless. Yunus has 416 poems, and only a few of them fall into the category of "riddles which appeared to be nonsensical."

The effort in Roditi and Dino's book to relate and compare the poetry of Yunus Emre to many elements and personages, including the false messiah Sabetay Sevi, might be useful in providing a comparative perspective, if only the same amount of effort had been spent on examining the relationship of Yunus Emre to Islam. One very revealing and significant example that shows the ethnocentric or ethnoreligious perspective and the flagrant lack of a basic knowledge of Islam occurs when the author comments on the following poem of Yunus Emre,

My friend came so often to see me
So long so many days and years
Willingly, would I be sacrificed
Like Ishmael in olden times

The following explanation is given: "The original Turkish text of this poem may moreover be corrupt, as a reference to the sacrifice of Isaac would seem more meaningful here than the existing one to the sacrifice of Ishmael."

Anyone who has a basic knowledge of Islam or has grown up in a Muslim society, indeed, anyone with the authority to write a book on Yunus Emre, knows that in Islamic tradition Ishmael is the son, not Isaac, who was to be sacrificed by Abraham. This is a minor, but still a very telling mistake. It represents the nucleus of the whole Orientalistic and ethnocentric perspective, which considers that everything which does not fit the expectations is corrupt, and the only meaningful thing is that which makes sense in a certain culture and to a certain group of people.

Kabir Helminski and Refik Algan, in *The Drop that Became the Sea,*[189] present Yunus Emre as "an illiterate peasant with a modest vocabulary,"[190] "the most important folk poet in the language of Islam,"[191] and "an inspired shepherd."[192] The idea of an unlettered shepherd is supported by some changes that have been made, showing Yunus Emre as 'foolish' in the legends. These changes are not found in written sources. One positive aspect of this book is that the translations of the poems were done in free verse and with a sense of the conversational idiom.

Another presentation of Yunus Emre in English, *The City of the Heart, Yunus Emre's Verses of Wisdom and Love,* provides a brief introduction and translation of 157 poems.[193] It should also be given credit for locating Yunus Emre in the context of the other Sufis of the time, such as Rumi.

The author of *The Poetry of Yunus Emre,* Grace Martin Smith, who translated ninety-five poems of Yunus Emre with a short introduction, is important in terms of presenting Yunus Emre as a product of "lively and progressive conditions" in Anatolia.[194] Yunus Emre generally has been seen to be a product of a world of chaos and warlike conditions created by internal struggles and Mongol invasions. Smith views him in the context of the rich cultural heritage of the Seljukids and the patronage of the Anatolian Turkish principalities. She describes the last years of Yunus Emre as "the best period of domination of Mongols."[195]

Smith describes the life and poetry of Yunus Emre without being judgmental or trying to show him as belonging to a specific group. Her brief analysis and consideration of Seljukid cultural heritage and the cultured and learned Mongol leadership result in a different portrait of Yunus Emre, which is hardly that of a "wandering fool."

Annemarie Schimmel, who is one of the most knowledgeable and complex scholars on Islamic mysticism, dealt with Yunus Emre in her *Mystical Dimensions of Islam*[196] under the title of "Turkish Popular Mysticism." Her treatment of Yunus Emre is notable for its insight and meticulous scholarship. However, there are several issues that could detract from the quality of her treatment and undermine many insightful perspectives that she introduces in the book.

Schimmel relates Yunus Emre to Rumi, Ahmed Yesevi and Sultan Walad, and states that "Yunus Emre stands in the tradition of classical Sufism,"[197] a term that she explains as mediating death, grounding one's faith firmly in the Qur'an, giving importance to ritual prayers as well as *dhikr*, being an ardent lover of Prophet Muhammad, etc. She also criticizes the modern Turkish interpreters of Yunus' poetry who tend to regard him as a representative of unorthodox Turkish national piety and says, "they forget how deeply rooted in the Muslim tradition is his mystical approach."[198] Along with this idea Schimmel explains some poems in which Yunus Emre calls himself Jesus, Moses or sometimes God, with the concept of a "cosmic consciousness."[199] She also discusses skillfully some of the classical and modern interpretations of the poetry of Yunus Emre. Up to this point, nothing can be criticized in her discussion of Yunus Emre. However, after this, Schimmel introduces Kaygusuz Abdal, a 17th century poet, who it is claimed used opium, and says, "One may ask how the poetry of Yunus and Kaygusuz can be explained in the framework of Sufism."[200] The tone of her language and this question create the impression that she has completed the descriptive part of the discussion and now is passing to the analytical part. At this point, she introduces "automatic writing," with a personal anecdote, as well as bringing up "spiritualist séances"[201] and "outwardly Islamicized Jewish converts."[202]

Schimmel concludes that "Yunus Emre [is] among the foremost masters of Bektaşi poetry" and "Muhammad, Ali, and the twelve imams of Shiite Islam figure prominently in this literature, as in the whole fabric of Bektaşi thought in which Allah, Muhammad, and Ali even constitute a sort of trinity."[203]

First of all, considering Yunus Emre as a Bektashi poet on the basis that some Bektashi poets in later centuries composed similar poems to that of Yunus is not a valid argument. It was not only Bektashis who composed poems like that of Yunus Emre; many other poets from various brotherhoods did the same, such as Niyazi Mısri, and Hacı Bayram Veli, who were both the leader of brotherhoods known by their names.

Secondly, calling Yunus Emre a Bektashi is an anachronism. Many scholars agree that until the fifteenth century there was no noteworthy Shiite influence, indeed not even a Shiite Islam presence in Anatolia. The name of the eldest son of the sheikh of Hacı Bektaş was Ömer, while one of leading students of this sheikh was called Osman, the names of the second and the third caliphs, which are not used by the Shiites.[204] Yunus could very well have been a Bektashi; however, he was also very respectful of the names of Prophet Muhammad, Abu Bakr, Ömer [or Umar] and Osman [or Uthman], who are not regarded well by Shiites or by some modern Bektashis.

Finally, in the poetry of Yunus Emre, it is impossible to find poems that suggest a Shiite perception of the universe or Islam. Ali is revered and mentioned, as is the case in many Sufi poets. One important issue is the fact that every time Ali is mentioned, either the Prophet or the other three caliphs are also mentioned.[205] Even in the works attributed to Hacı Bektaş Veli, the founder of the Bektashi order, we do not see a full-fledged Shiite Islam, if we see any at all.

Sezai Karakoç (b.1933), a poet and intellectual, published a slim book in 1965 called *Yunus Emre* in which he evaluates Yunus Emre as a poet who adapted the religion of Islam into the language of poetry and made it available to Turks. He considers Yunus Emre the founding spirit of the Ottoman state and society. He says, "...just as the German invasion symbolized in *The Plague* by Camus gave birth to a philosophy and literature of resistance in France, just as Camus's absurdism and Sartre's existentialism appeared in a moment of life and death, Anatolia was able to protect itself with a metaphysical move and establish itself with a great historical presence."[206]

Karakoç discusses previous scholarship and warns the reader that "[this period] is studied either from the perspective of dusty Orientalists or from the perspective of biased Babalık-Dedelik [referring to the heterodox interpretation of Yunus Emre], as if the goal is not to find the reality of this age but to look for a possibility of and reason for the existence of certain petty heresies."[207] He opposes the idea of Ali accusing the other Companions of the Prophet and suggests that in the beginning there were no heretical elements in the Bektashi order. Otherwise, he continues, the Ottomans, who were very sensitive about these issues, would not have allowed them to be influential in military institutions. He argues that the teachings of Hacı Bektaş were changed because of political reasons related to Iran, such as migrations to Anatolia, enmity toward the state, and the idea of connecting ancient beliefs and motifs to a great personality.[208] He also suggests that the work of Yunus Emre should be viewed in its totality, not individually, and that every single poem should be interpreted by keeping in mind the fact that it was part of a bigger reality.[209]

Karakoç's work is not a scholarly work and he does not claim it to be such. However, he has a very interesting and insightful perspective and in many cases follows historical realities, such as the establishment of the Bektashi order and the political and social reasons behind later developments, for the various Alevite-Bektashi groups.

Anthologies have played an important role in shaping the popular reception of Yunus Emre. In the anthologies that I have been able to access there are two noticeable patterns that are relevant to the reception of Yunus Emre: The first one is the nature of the poems selected for inclusion in the anthology, which are overwhelmingly easy to understand for Turkish-speaking people in the 20th century. There might have been various criteria for the people who prepared these anthologies and their reasons might have been subjective. However, one can easily argue that the selection of poems did not present a good representation of the body of Yunus Emre's poetry. For instance, in Asım Bezirci's anthology[210] there is not a single word that might be difficult for a 20th century speaker of Turkish, although there are many words in the poems of Yunus Emre that cannot be understood even by educated Turks. Similarly, all of the fourteen poems in Sunullah Arısoy's anthology[211] are relatively easy to understand as well as those in the work by Ali Püsküllüoğlu.[212]

The second pattern to be noticed in these anthologies is the phonetic and lexical modernization of the poems. In the texts, the fourteenth century phonetic features of the words, such as *içerü, adlu*, and *işk*, are ignored and the poems are presented as a contemporary text.

These two patterns, accompanied by the idea that Yunus Emre was a folk poet, as implied in titling these anthologies "folk poetry," an assertion expressed by Birge in the title of his 1933 article,[213] creates the false impression that Yunus Emre was purely a folk poet and therefore different from other poets, such as Hoca Dehhani or Ahmedi, who are considered to be early representatives of Ottoman court poetry.

Yunus Emre is portrayed as the main protagonist or secondary figure in many works of fiction as well. There are two novels that can be considered to be fictional biographies of Yunus Emre. The first novel was published in 1990 by Mustafa Necati Sepetçioğlu (b. 1932), the author of many historical novels.[214] In this novel, the most visible issue is the foundation of the Ottoman state with the cooperation of dervishes and statesmen. The thesis of the novel is very much like that of Barkan's, which considers dervishes to be the founders of Ottoman society. Yunus Emre is a representative of the dervishes who came to Anatolia and the period and geography are provided through his inner dialogue. According to the novel, dervishes played a vital role after the catastrophic events caused by the Mongols, helping to return society back to its normal mode.

The second novel, *Bir Ben Vardır Bende Benden İçeri,*[215] published in 2002, is by Emine Işınsu (b.1938), the daughter of another author, Halide Nusret Zorlutuna (1901–1984). Although there are serious linguistic problems with the language of the novel[216] and the author sometimes is clearly presenting a 20th century perspective to 14th century life, the novel is very successful, particularly in depicting the dilemma of Yunus Emre caught between the material world and the spiritual world. Işınsu seems to understand the mystical stations and successfully applies them to the novel's setting. The presentation of Yunus both as a man of flesh and blood and as a man of heart and Divine love are very successfully carried out. Işınsu's 20th century perspective can be observed, particularly in the portrayal of Yunus Emre as a child. Yunus Emre is portrayed as child who was very conscious about using the Turkish language and being very strict about not studying the Qur'an unless he understood what the verses meant.[217]

CONCLUSION

The idea that Yunus Emre was a product of dark, unstable times, and that his poetry is the result and reflection of this era has no historical basis. Rather, Yunus Emre inherited a rich, complex cultural legacy from the last period of the Seljukid state, as clearly demonstrated by the ideas and references in his poetry and by the archival works regarding this period. Rather than labeling him a wandering dervish without a clear purpose, Yunus Emre should be considered to be part of an organized movement that cultivated and helped the foundation of the Ottoman state and its culture.

The cultural texture of the poetry of Yunus Emre demonstrates that we must take Sufism into consideration when interpreting his poetry; in this period, Sufism was at its peak, and included among its adherents such great Muslim figures as Ibn Arabi, Rumi, Fakhruddin Iraqi, and Qushayri. Also at this time there was a tremendous amount of cultural, social, and religious interaction in Anatolia. Yunus Emre is the product of this cultural world. He should not be interpreted as a simple folk poet, rather, he should be seen to be a poet who masterfully digested this complex and rich web of ideas and presented it in a way that could be attractive to the Turkish speaking masses, as well as to highly educated people of his time.

The textual and historical sources do not provide definitive conclusions about the brotherhood to which Yunus Emre belonged. The evidence used to defend his ties with the Bektashi or Qalandari orders is either taken out of context or is too broad to argue the case for membership in a specific brotherhood. However, the discussions of whether he was a Bektashi or not shed light on another issue, which is how the concept of the Bektashi order was treated in literary and even historical works. In these discussions, the historical dual development of the Bektashi order as eastern Bektashis and western Bektashis is subsumed under a post–1826 Bektashi development, which is dominantly anti-Ottoman. Yunus Emre certainly could be called a Bektashi, however one has to remember the historical distinction between western Bektashis and eastern Bektashis, both politically and theologically.

Yunus Emre shared a very similar cultural environment with Rumi, Ibn Arabi, Fakhruddin Iraqi and Najmuddin Kubra. Mostly because of literary historical writings with a national bias and a lack of interest in other languages, there are not many cross-linguistic studies that focus on figures who shared the same cultural environment but used different languages to express their messages. One has to consider the works of these men in order to place Yunus Emre within the atmosphere of broader trends in Islamic intellectual history, as well as local, linguistic, regional distinctions.

The place of poetry during the age of Yunus Emre and the major themes in his poetry are crucial for understanding his work. Yunus Emre and many Sufi poets of the time composed poetry to spread their message, using their poetic talent as dervishes in the best possible way, in the service of God; that is, their interest was didactical, not one of belles lettres. The themes that Yunus Emre covered in his poetry, such as divine love, the idea of death and the transitory nature of the world, the unity of being or Divine consciousness, perfected human beings, and themes of a didactic nature coincide with the themes in the works of other major figures of the time, such as Rumi, Ahmed Yesevi, Iraqi, and Ibn Arabi, as well as general Sufi religious philosophy.

The language Yunus Emre used in his poetry demonstrates that he did not avoid words of Persian or Arabic origin. He used as many Persian and Arabic words as Turkish, as well as the Arabo-Persian meter of Ottoman court poetry and Turkish meters and forms, such as *koşma*. Interestingly, both in the case of the linguistic origins of the words and in the case of forms and meters, Yunus Emre used both without choosing one at the expense of the other. It would be wrong to present him as a poet who limited himself to the use of Turkish words or Turkish forms in his poetry. One also has to consider that understanding the literal meanings of the words does not enable one to understand the poetry of Yunus Emre.

However, the discussions around the linguistic origins of the words used in his poetry should not overshadow Yunus Emre's unprecedented success and power in terms of expressing the most complex ideas and most vivid images in powerfully beautiful language. He is the poet who expressed the relationship between human beings, the world and God in a most powerful way in Turkish. He created and developed Sufi terminology in Turkish, either by coining new words and phrases or by accommodating Persian and Arabic ones within Turkish.

Yunus Emre was well appreciated and known among the various classes, as the sources indicate. Those who attempt to show that there were enmities between various social groups in Ottoman society can find no evidence to support their claims in Yunus Emre's poetry. Rather, he appears to be a unifying figure and a clear example appreciated by Sufis from different orders.

In the modern period the reception of Yunus Emre has been grossly distorted by various factors. The attempts to create a cultural past for Turkish nationalism, to present Yunus Emre to an audience in order to deconstruct the image of the terrible Turk, to create divisions by constructing unsubstantiated dichotomies (Ottoman elite versus Ottoman masses, center versus periphery, heterodox versus orthodox orders, Islam versus pre-Islamic culture or ancient Anatolian civilizations), and attempts by Orientalists to claim Yunus Emre's positive aspects were derived from Christianity are all major factors in distorting the perception of him and his work. One can see in these approaches the effect of negative notions regarding Islam both in the West and in Turkey. Yunus Emre was a Sufi who defined himself within the Muslim tradition and whose poetry reflects this reality with great clarity.

A Selection of Poems from Yunus Emre's *Divan*

A SELECTION OF POEMS FROM YUNUS EMRE'S *DIVAN**

XXIX

Not talking at all is the best way to talk,
Talking is the dirt of souls.

In order to wash and be rid of this dirt,
Speak the word which is the essence of all words.

Even to the one who always speaks the truth, God said, "Say the truth"
The one who speaks falsely today shall be ashamed of lying tomorrow.

The one who does not consider all people the same
Might be a saint in law but is a rebel in reality.

Let me speak of the nature of Law and reality,
Law is the ship and reality the sea.

No matter how strong the planks of the ship,
When the waves of the sea stroke it, the ship is overcome.

Those who are desolate in the world
Abandon reason, soul, understanding, heart and thought.

We are students and we constantly study the course of love;
God assigns the course and love itself is the teacher.

O beloved! Let me tell you something about reality of the things,
The infidel in reality is the saint of law.

Since Geyikli Baba[1] once gazed upon us,
I have taken whatever is my share.

---

* Turkish originals of the poems are in Mustafa Tatçı (ed.), *Yunus Emre Divanı*, vol. II. (1990 edition).

XXXIII

Abandon the fear of dying; lovers do not die, they are eternal,
You have nothing to do with dying, your soul is Divine.

Why are you afraid of death? Do not be afraid, you will exist forever.
Why are you afraid of death? It is an empty thought.

Take a look at this jewel, and this hidden light,
Where does the light go? That is the place where God looks.

Thank God! He is the One Who is eternal,
You will go to Him anyway! Go to Him thankfully.

We knew each other from primordial times,
Do not look at this body; it is just a container for the soul.

This primordial unity and this peace of the universe,
This unity of souls is the extension of Divine might.

Those who know there is no strangeness should be peaceful for the newcomers
For those who are self-righteous the path to unity is very steep.

The judge of the land knows best,
This land is the house of existence.

Yunus, good news for you; they say "Come towards God,"
The essence of the word is "everything goes back to its origin."

XLIX

God has given me a spirit which becomes admiring in an instant;
You see it becomes happy and then it becomes sad.

You think it is like winter; it is like the coldest month;
Then you see that it is good news and it becomes like a joyful garden.

It cannot speak a single word, nor explain anything;
Then you see it is speaking pearls and curing the sick.

It rises into the sky and then it goes underground;
You think it is a drop and then it overflows and becomes an ocean.

It lies in ignorance and knows not a single word;
Then it dives deep into wisdom and becomes Calinus or Luqman.

It becomes like a giant or an ogre and dwells in the ruins;
Then it flies with Balqis[2] and becomes the sultan of humans and jinn.

You see that it has become a beggar in coarse cloth;
Then, with a generous blessing, it becomes like a sultan or emperor.

It becomes rebellious, and God lets it lose its mind;
Then piety and belief become its company.

It thinks of its sins and faces Hell directly;
Then it envisions the mercy of God and looks forward to Heaven.

It goes to the mosques and prostrates;
Then it goes into a church, reads the Bible and becomes a priest.

It becomes like Moses and prays a thousand times;
Then it enters the sphere of arrogance and becomes like the Pharaoh and Haman.[3]

It brings the dead to life like Jesus;
Then it loses its balance and becomes rebellious.

It becomes like Gabriel and spreads mercy everywhere;
Then it gets lost and poor Yunus admires it.

LXVI

Listen O friends! Love is like a sun;
A heart without love is like a stone.

Whatever comes out of a heart with no love, the tongue of that heart is poisonous;
No matter how softly he speaks, his words are warlike.

If there is love, the heart burns; it softens like a candle.
Stone hearts are like darkened, steppe-cold winter.

In the presence of that sultan, in the gate of that great person,
The star of lovers is always like Venus.

Love is the bellows; it stirs the blood of lovers.
It smelts them, pouring through many molds and making them silver.

The lover's spirit is not satisfied unless it finds the Beloved.
It cannot stay in the world but flies around like a bird.

An unbeliever does not know what he says; his words do not last long.
How can you interpret them? They are like disordered dreams.

Do not worry, Yunus, this way is not necessary,
What a man needs first is love, then he will look like a dervish.

XCI

Knowledge is to come to know yourself.
If you do not know yourself, what good is your knowledge?

The point of studying is to come to know God,
If one studies and still is not aware of God, studying is useless.

Do not brag about how much you studied or how much you prayed;
If you don't know God, all you did was in vain.

The entire meaning of the four Books[4] is in a single *alif*;
You read the *alif*, but what is its meaning?

Yunus Emre says, even if you go on pilgrimage a thousand times,
It would be much better to gain one's heart.

CI

If one knows how to use the word, the word makes that person proud.
If one speaks carefully, the word makes the work best.

There are words that stop war and there are words that make the dead live.
There are words that make a poisonous dish a delicacy.

Choose your words carefully and sift out the bad ones;
Speak in a good manner and do not speak like a child.

O brother, come and listen to my word;
One word makes thousands of jewels worthless.

One has to know the manner of the word, and not use bad words.
One word makes this hellish world like Heaven.

Walk in a good way; do not be unaware of wisdom.
Be careful! A single word can harm your soul.

O Yunus! Now speak in a good manner, speak the best of words.
Be careful! A single word can keep you away from His presence.

CXXIV

The paths of saints are finer than a hair;
It was an ant that blocked Suleiman's way.

That ant spoke and taught a way to Suleiman;
When the ant spoke, it got a response.

No burdened soul bears the burden of another;
Those who say they did are certainly lying.

Whoever is careless of whether he says something good or bad to another
God will punish him; this is a delicate issue.

CXXV

I used to complain about my suffering but I have found the cure in my suffering,
I used to long for my Friend and my Friend is secretly present nearby.

Wherever I was I used to contemplate; I used to look at the sky and give thanks.
I used to long for my Friend and my Friend is secretly present nearby.

I used to think that I had an independent existence but I am one and my Friend is the other.
My thinking like this was because I was a human being.

The aspects of God are in human beings if you can see rightly;
The entire universe admires the features of human beings.

Whoever knows the human being becomes a real human being, even if he is a beast.
The human being is the sultan over all the creatures.

The whole unity represents a unity; the one who realizes this unity is called a human being.
The one who denies this unity is an enemy of himself.

The one who is a human being finds God and he has the Sufi gathering, O Giver of wine;
This helpless Yunus has become familiar with love.

CLXVI

If you have broken a heart even once, your prayers are of no use.
Of all the nations of the world, none can have respect for you.

Friends of God came and are gone; they have all left the world and passed away.
They flew to the sky; they are like birds of paradise, not like geese.

What I call the soul is the one that reaches God; what I call feet are those that reach the path.
What I call a real man is the one who is humble; whoever is haughty is not worthy.

Those who deny, and those who make claims, those who are picky about details;
It is they who deserve to live in a barn if they seek not love.

If you have taken the right path, if you have followed a real human being,
If you have committed a good deed, then this deserves a thousand things.

Yunus sets up these words as if mixing butter with honey,
He sells his load to people, and his load is jewelry not salt.

CLXXIX

I am not permanent here; I came here to leave.
I am a merchant with many goods that I came to sell.

I did not come to fight, I came for love.
The house of the Friend is the heart; I came to heal hearts.

My madness is because of the friend; those who are in love understand.
Changing this duality, I came to reach oneness.

He is my teacher and I am his servant; I am the nightingale of the garden of the Friend.
In the garden of the Friend, I came to be happy and sing.

Those who cannot know each other here, cannot know each other in the Hereafter.
I came here to become acquainted with my friend and to explain my situation.

Yunus Emre has fallen in love and has died of love.
I came to explain my situation at the gate of the true friend.

CCXXXI

We are about to leave the world, greetings to those who have stayed here;
Greetings to those who pray for us.

Death will bend our backs and stop our tongues from speaking;
Greetings to those who ask about our situation when we are unwell.

My body will come out; a shirt with no neck will be fashioned;
Greetings to those who wash our body in a pure way.

The Angel of Death takes my soul and my blood dries up in its veins;
Greetings to those who wind us in our shroud.

We are about to go to our friends and we could not reach our goal;
Greetings to those who stand for our funeral prayers.

The word is recounted in vain and nobody can endure this trouble;
Greetings to those who put us into the grave.

In this world, all who come leave and do not return;
Greetings to those who ask for news of our situation.

The one who loves God and the one who seeks remedy in the suffering from God is the lover;
Greetings to those who pray for us.

Helpless Yunus utters the words; his eyes are filled with bloody tears.
How can those who do not know us know us? Greetings to those who know us.

CCLXX

You are flooded, O crazy soul! Are you raging like rivers?
Once again you shed my bloody tears! Will you stop me?

What can I do? I cannot reach my Beloved! No cure for my illness,
I have stayed away from my true home! Will you keep me here?

I have lost my companion! The pain of my soul does not abate.
O bloody tears of my eyes! Will you rage like rivers?

I became dirt on your path; you look for other things.
Are you stone mountains stretched out in front of me?

O snowy mountain that bars my way like a highway robber.
I am parted from my beloved; will you still block my way?

O tresses of cloud on top of the snowy mountains,
Will you untie your hair and shed tears for me?

The soul of Yunus became ecstatic; I am on the path to my home.
Yunus saw you in his dream, are you in good health or ill?

CCLXXI

I have found the soul of souls; let my soul be looted,
I gave up loss or profit; let my store be looted.

I gave up my ego, I got rid of the curtain over my eyes,
I reached the unity of God; let my doubts be looted.

My ego left me, my Friend occupied all my lands,
I became a man of no land; let my lands be looted.

I became weary of duality, I put on the robe of love,
I have reached the source of grief; let my cures be looted.

He strived for the creation, and because of this the Friend came to us,
My ruined heart was filled with light; let my universe be looted.

I gave up never-ending desires, I became weary of winters and summers,
I found the head of the gardens; let my garden be looted.

I am tired of relations, I have flown to the side of that Friend,
I fell into the council of love; let my own council be looted.

O Yunus! How sweetly you have spoken, as if you have eaten honey and sugar,
I have found the best of the honey; let my beehives be looted.

CCXCIX

Real manliness is from modesty,
If one is arrogant, he will soon fall.

The soul travels very high, deviates now and then from the path,
Whatever is inside leaks out.

A white-bearded old man, he cannot recognize his situation;
There is no point going on pilgrimage if he has broken a heart.

A senseless man does not hear the word, he confuses day with night;
Even if the universe is lit up, the deniers' eyes are blind.

The heart is the crown of God; God looks at the crown,
Whoever breaks a heart is miserable in both worlds.

Whatever you think of yourself, you should think the same of others,
This is the true meaning of the four holy Books.

We understood that everybody who came has left and moved away,
The ones who find meaning are those drunk with the wine of love.

May Yunus not deviate from the path, let him not be arrogant,
May he not see the grave and the *sirat* bridge if he is in love with the "face" of God.

CCCLXXXI

Your love has taken me from me,
I need You, only You.
I burn day and night,
I need You, only You.

Neither do I rejoice at existing
Nor do I feel regret at not existing.
I am consoled by Your love,
I need You, only You.

Your love kills the lovers,
Your love makes people dive into the sea of love,
Your love fills one up with manifestation,
I need You, only You.

Let me break the chain of love,
Let me be crazy and go to the mountains,
You are my thought day and night,
I need You, only You.

If they kill me,
Scatter my ashes in the air.
My dust will call that
I need You, only You.

Sufis need conversation
Those after the Hereafter need the Hereafter
Majnuns need their Leylas,
I need You, only You.

Neither a place in Hell took I,
Nor reserved I a pavilion in Heaven.
Much have I cried for You,
I need You, only You.

What they call Heaven
Is a few houses and *houris*
Give them to those who want them,
I need You, only You.

Appendixes

APPENDIXES

APPENDIX I

Ben bende seyr eder iken acep sırra irdüm ahi
Bir siz dahi siz de görün dostu bende gördüm ahi

Bende baktım bende gördüm benumile ben olanı
Suretüme can olanı kimdügüni bildim ahi

Ben istedüm buldum anı ol ben isem ya ben kani
Seçemedim andan beni bir kezden ol oldum ahi

Suret topraktır diyeni gönlüm kabul itmez ani
Bu toprağın cevherini Hazrete irgürdüm ahi

Münkir kişi duymaz ani dertlülerin sizer cani
Ben dost bağı bülbüleyem ol bağçeden geldim ahi

Maşuk bizimledür bile ayru değül kuldan kula
Uzak sefer bizden kala dosti yakın buldum ahi

Değme bir yol kandan bana tağılmayan değme yana
Kutlu oldu bu seferüm hoş menzile irdum ahi

Mansur idim ben ol zaman us yine geldim bunda ben
Yak kulumı savur yile ben ana'l Hak didim ahi

Ne oda yanam dağılam ne dara çıkam boğılam
İşüm bitince yüriyem teferrüce geldüm ahi

Münim oldum yoksul iken benüm oldu kevn u mekan
Şarka vü Garba ser-te-ser yire göğe doldum ahi

Nitekim ben beni bildüm dilediğüm Hakk'ı buldum
Korkim anı buluncadı korkidan kurtuldum ahi

Yunus kim öldürür seni viren alur tatlı cani
Bu canlara hükm ideni kim idüğün bildim ahi

(Yunus Emre, II, 470)

Appendix II

Işkun aldı benden beni bana seni gerek seni
Ben yanaram düni güni bana seni gerek seni

Ne varlığa sevinirim ne yokluğa yirinürem
Işkunila avunurum bana seni gerek seni

Işkun aşıklar öldürür ışk denizine daldırır
Tecelliyle doldurur bana seni gerek seni

Işkun zincirini üzem delü olam daga düşem
Sensün din ü gün endişem bana seni gerek seni

Eğer beni öldüreler külüm göğe savuralar
Toprağım anda çağıra bana seni gerek seni

Sufilere sohbet gerek ahilere ahret gerek
Mecnunlara Leyla gerek bana seni gerek seni

Ne Tamuda yir eyledim ne Uçmakda köşk bağladum
Senin için çok ağladım bana seni gerek sen

Cennet cennet dedikleri bir ev ile bir kaç huri
İsteyene virgil anı bana seni gerek seni

Yusuf eğer hayalini düşte göreydi bir gece
Terk ideyidi mülklerin bana seni gerek seni

Yunus çağırırlar adım gün geçtikçe artar odum
İki cihanda maksudum bana seni gerek seni

(Yunus Emre, II, 383–384)

Appendix III

Cihandan ben usanmışam bana seni gerek seni
Kamulardan üşenmişem bana seni gerek seni

Niderem ben ten ü canı ya sensuz abı hayvanı
Veyahud din ü imanı bana seni gerek seni

Gerekmez ravh ile rıdvan gerekmez hur ile vildan
Gerekmez ravza-i rıdvan bana seni gerek seni

Gerekmez gönlüme selvet gerekmez ruhuma rahat
Gerekmez canuma işret bana seni gerek seni

Gerekmez milket-i dünya gerekmez devlet-i ukba
Gerekmez kevser-i tuba bana seni gerek seni

İçüm sensiz cehennemdir yaşum ile cihan nemdir
Benüm sensiz cihan nemdür bana seni gerek seni

Dilenmez Ahmedi ey şeyh ki onun ola mihr ü meh
Bu iki kevnde billah bana seni gerek seni.

Ahmedi (Gölpınarlı, *Yunus Emre ve Tasavvuf*, 232)

Appendix IV

Keleci bilen kişinin yüzünü ağ ede bir söz
Sözü bişirüp diyenin işini sağede bir söz

Söz ola kese savaşı söz ola bitire bitüre başı
Söz ola ağulu aşı balile yağ ede bir söz

Kelecilerün bişirgil yaramazunı şeşürgül
Sözün usula düşürgil dimegil çağ ide bir söz

Gel ahi ey şehriyarı sözümüzü dinle bari
Hezar gevher u dinari kara toprağ ide bir söz

Kişi bile soz demini dimeye sozun kemini
Bu cihan cehennemini sekiz ucmak ede bir soz

Yüri yüri yolunula gafil olma bilinüle
Key sakın key dilinüle canına dağ ede bir soz

Yunus imdi söz yatından söyle sözi gayetinden
Key sakın o she katından seni ırağ ide bir soz

(Yunus Emre, II, 113–114)

Appendix V

Sözünü bir söyleyenin sözünü sağ eder bir söz
Pir nefesi dinleyenün yüzünü eder ağ bir söz

Bir söz vardır halk içinde dahi söz var hulk içinde
Olmaya ki delk içinde diyesin çarkadağ bir söz

Söz vardur kesdurur başı söz vardur keser savaşı
Söz vardur agulu aşı balilan ede yağ bir söz

Sözini yahşi bişürgil yahşi usilna düşürgil
Yaramazunı sesirgil canuna olur dağ bir söz

İsterem göreyim yari bu remzi anlagil vari
Hezaran ehl-i ikrarı eder kara toprağ bir söz

Şah Hatayi ayatundan sözün söyle öz zatundan
Olmaya kim pir katundan seni ırağ ede bir söz

Şah İsmail, (Gölpınarlı, *Yunus Emre ve Tasavvuf*, 236)

Notes

INTRODUCTION

1 The translations of Yunus Emre's works and studies on his work and life in other languages are: in English, J. Kingsley Birge, "*Yunus Emre, Turkey's Great Poet of the People*," *The Macdonald Presentation Volume* (Princeton: Princeton University, 1933); Talat S. Halman, *Poetry of Yunus Emre* (Istanbul: Istanbul Matbaası, 1972); *Yunus Emre and His Mystical Poetry*, Talat S. Halman (ed.), (Bloomington: Indiana University Press, 1981); Eduardo Roditi and Güzin Dino, *Yunus Emre, The Wandering Fool: Sufi Poems of a 13th Century Dervish* (San Francisco: Cadmus Editions, 1987); Kebir Helminski and Refik Algan, *The Drop that Became the Sea* (Vermont: Threshold Books, 1989); Ahmet Edip Uysal, *International 1991 Yunus Emre Year of Love* (Ankara: Ministry of Culture, 1991); Süha Faiz, The *City of the Heart, Yunus Emre's Verses of Wisdom and Love,* preface by John D. Norton (Massachusetts: Elements, 1992); Grace Martin Smith, *The Poetry of Yunus Emre* (Berkeley, Los Angeles and London: University of California Press, 1993); *Yunus Emre, Spiritual Experience and Culture,* International Seminar, Rome, November 6-9, 1991, Gregorian University and University of Ankara. (Roma: Editrice Potitificia Universita Gregoriana, 1994). In French, Said Khourshid, *La langue de Yunus Emre Contribution à L'Histoire du Turc pre-Ottoman (*Ankara: Editions Ministere de La Culture, 1991); Bedreddin Tuncel, *Yunus Emre, Occasion du 750eme anniversaire de sa naissance* (Paris: Edition Publisud, 1991); Mevlüt Bozdemir, *Yunus Emre, Message Universel* (Paris: Inalco, 1992). In German, Annemarie Schimmel, *Wanderungen mit Yunus Emre* (Koln: Onel, 1989); Annemarie Schimmel, *Ausgewahlte Gedichte von Yunus Emre* (Koln: Onel, 1991). In Urdu, Yunas Imriyah: Turki da Azim avami shaer by Talat S. Halman (Islamabad: Ilaqai Saqafati Idarah, 1971). In Albanian, Musa Kraja, Nexhip P. Alpan, *Jonuz Emre, poet dhe educator i madh popullor* (Tirane: Shtepia Botuese Koha, 1999). In Russian, Sh. V. Gabeskiriia, *Leksika Proizvedenii: Iunusa Emre* (Tbilisi: Izd-vo Metsniereba, 1983); Vladimir Borisovich Kudelin, *Poeziia Iunusa Emre: K voprosu o gumanizme v literature srednikh vekov* (Moskva: Nauka, 1980).

2 In a Yunus Emre bibliography prepared in 1988 by Mustafa Tatçı and Suzan Gürelli there are more than 1,000 works on Yunus Emre. See Mustafa Tatçı and Suzan Gürelli, *Yunus Emre Bibliyografyası* (Ankara: Kültür ve Turizm Bakanlığı, 1988).

3 *Divan* [also *Diwan*] is a collection of poems by a single author; it can consist of either selected works or the entire corpus of the poet.

Chapter 1: The Age in Which Yunus Emre Lived and His Place in the Sufi Tradition of His Time

1 See Abdülbaki Gölpınarlı, *Yunus Emre ve Tasavvuf* (Istanbul: Remzi, 1961), p. 8. Tanpınar also makes a comparison between Yunus Emre and Prophet Jonah, referring to the time of the Mongols as a dark era that was similar to the time that Jonah spent in the belly of the fish. Ahmet Hamdi Tanpınar, *Edebiyat Üzerine Makaleler,* ed. by Zeynep Kerman (Istanbul: Dergah, 1977), pp. 134–135; Sebahattin Eyüboğlu, *Yunus Emre* (Istanbul: Cem, 1980), p. 22.

2 Claude Cahen, *Pre-Ottoman Turkey: a general survey of the material and spiritual culture and history c. 1071–1330;* translated from the French [manuscript] by J. Jones-Williams (London, Sidgwick & Jackson, 1968), p. 347. See also: Al-Ahri, *Tarikh-i Shaikh Uwais,* edited and translated by J.B.Van Loon (The Hague: Uitgeverij Excelsior, 1954), p. 51.

3 The Ilkhanid state was founded in 1256 by Genghis Khan's grandson Hulagu in Iran, with Tabriz as the center. The Mongols destroyed and sacked the cities which were the scientific, cultural, and commercial centers of Anatolia. By the time they had defeated the Anatolian Seljukid state, the Ilkhanids had undergone a transformation, and during the reign of the Ilkhanid Ghazan Mahmud Khan (1295–1303) they embraced Islam—the religion professed by most of the people living in its territories.

4 Cahen, p. 348.

5 Fakhruddin Iraqi, *Divine Flashes*, translated by William Chittick and Peter Lamborn Wilson. Preface by Seyyed Husain Nasr (New York: Paulist Press, 1982), p. 59; Osman Turan, *Selçuklular Zamanında Türkiye*, (Istanbul: Turan Neşriyat Yurdu, 1971), p. 482.

6 Cahen, p. 318.

7 Ibid., p. 133.

8 The case of the origin of *akhi*s is a good example of nationalist historiography. Some scholars such as Neşet Çağatay ignore the fact that this institution existed in other Muslim countries such as Syria, Iraq, Persia, Andalusia and Egypt and consider this institution to be a Turkish innovation, emphasizing Ahi Evran, who lived in Anatolia at the end of Seljukid period. See Neşet Çağatay, *Bir Türk Kurumu Olarak Ahilik* (Ankara: Ankara Üniversitesi, 1974). For the prior forms of the same institution see: *Türkiye Diyanet Vakfi İslam Ansiklopedisi*, 1st ed., s.v. "Ahilik"

9 The Hanafi, Shafii, Maliki, and Hanbali schools are the four schools of *fiqh*, or religious law, within Sunni Islam.

10 Osman Turan, *Selçuklular ve İslamiyet*, p. 20.

11 Tatçı, *Yunus Emre,* v.1, pp. 3–4.

12 Fakhruddin Iraqi: *Divine Flashes*, translated by William C. Chittick and Peter Lamborn Wilson, preface by Seyyed Hossein Nasr, (New York: Paulist Press, 1982), p. 59.

13 Seffattin Severcan, *Alaaddin Keykubat (1220–1237) devrine ait Necmeddin Daye'nin Siyasetnamesi* (Kayseri: Erciyes, 1995).

14 İbrahim Hakkı Konyalı, *Abideleri ve Kitabeleriyle Konya Tarihi*, (Konya: Yeni Kitap Basımevi, 1964); Ethel Sara Wolper, "Princess Safwat al-Dunya wa al-Din and the Production of Sufi Buildings and Hagiographies in Pre-Ottoman Anatolia," in *Women, Patronage and Self-Representation in Islamic Societies,* edited by D. Fairchild Ruggles, (Albany: SUNY Press, 2000), pp. 35–52; Ethel Sara Wolper, *"The Politics and Patronage: Political Change and Construction of Dervish Lodges in Sivas"* Muqarnas 12 (1995): pp. 39–47.

15 Cahen, pp. 257–260.

16 Yunus Emre mentions Rumi's name and holds him in high regard. He even mentions that he joined Rumi's gatherings. Yunus Emre, II, p. 308. However, it is possible that the word "gathering" was used metaphorically, as is often the case in many Sufi texts.

17 Only a few of Ibn Arabi's works have been translated into English. However, the works of William C. Chittick are excellent guides, as well as the following translations into English: Ibn al Arabi, *Fusus al-Hikam*, English translation by R.W.J Austin, *Ibn al Arabi: The Bezels of Wisdom,* Ramsey (NJ: Paulist Press, 1981); Ibn al-Arabi, *Tarjuman al Ashwaq,* Edited and translated by R. A. Nicholson, *The Tarjuman al Ashwaq: A Collection of Mystical Odes by Muhyiddin ibn al Arabi* (London: Theosophical Publishing House, 1978).

18 The best work on this issue was published in 1942 by Ömer Lütfi Barkan, "Osmanlı İmparatorlugunda Bir İskan ve Kolonizasyon Metodu Olarak Vakıflar ve Temlikler I İstila Devirlerinin Kolonizatör Türk Dervişleri ve Zaviyeler," *Vakıflar Dergisi,* 1942, II, pp. 279–386.

19 The annual income of the Seljukid state was 17,000,000 gold pieces. In the same period the annual income of France was 3,000,000 and that of England was 4,000,000. W. Bartold, Ilhaniler Devrinde Mali Vaziyet, T.H.I.T. Mecmuası, I, 107 quoted in Osman Turan, *Selçuklular ve İslamiyet,* pp. 67–68.

20 Cahen, p. 317.

21 Osman Turan, *Selçuklular ve İslamiyet,* p. 20.

22 For critical scholarship on this issue see: Ahmet Yaşar Ocak, "Türkiye'de Ahilik Araştırmalarına Eleştirel Bir Bakış" in *Türk Sufiliğine Bakışlar* (Istanbul: İletişim, 1996), pp. 169–190.

23 Rumi, quoted in Annemarie Schimmel, *I am Wind, You are Fire*, *The Life and Work of Rumi (*Boston: Shambala, 1992), p. 40.

24 A recent article challenges this idea: Ahmet Arı, "Persian Poetry or Poetry in Persian? Thoughts about Formation and Boundaries of Classical Turkish Poet-

ry Custom." *Bilig, Journal of Social Sciences of Turkish World,* Winter, 2003, pp. 173–203.

25 The anecdotes of Nasreddin Hodja have been translated into English: Shah Idris, *The Subtleties of the Inimitable Mulla Nasruddin,* (London: Octagon, 1973); *Watermelons, Walnuts, and the Wisdom of Allah, and other tales of the Hoca,* translated by Barbara K. Walker and Harold Berson (New York: Parents' Magazine Press, 1967). It is interesting that the first work in the modern period on Nasreddin Hodja was written by Fuat Köprülü, who also wrote *First Mystics in Turkish Literature* and introduced Yunus Emre as a Turkish poet. A similar approach can be seen in this work, too. Fuat Köprülü, *Nasreddin Hoca* (Istanbul: Kanaat Matbaası ve Kütüphanesi, 1918). Another interesting case that uses the Hoca [Hodja] anecdotes to carry Sufi messages is Doris Lessing (1943-1996) a fiction writer. See: Müge Galin, *Between East and West, Sufism in the Novels of Doris Lessing* (Albany: SUNY Press, 1997).

26 Hasan al-Basri, for instance, makes mention of the term "Sufi." Al-Basri, who personally knew many of the Companions of the Prophet said: "I saw a Sufi circumambulating the Ka'ba and offered him something, but he would not take it, saying, 'I have four *daniq*s; what I have suffices me'" (at-Tusi, *Kitab al-Luma' fi at-Tasawwuf*, p. 42).

27 Carl Ernst, *Shambala Guide to Sufism*, (Boston: Shambala, 1997).

28 In 1914 Reynold A. Nicholson, who is one of the most quoted scholars in works on Sufism in the English language, wrote: "We have often noticed the difficulty in which the Sufis find themselves when they try to make a logical compromise with Islam. But the word logic is very misleading in this connexion. The beginning of wisdom for European students of Oriental religion lies in the discovery that incongruous beliefs—I mean, of course, beliefs which *our* minds cannot harmonize—dwell peacefully together in the Oriental brain... Contradictions which seem glaring to us do not trouble him at all." *The Mystics of Islam* (London: Routledge, 1970), [First published in 1914], p. 130. It is clear that the author considers Islam and Sufism as independent entities. The racist dichotomy of "we" and "they" and "Oriental brain" are also significant to demonstrate the direction and fundamentals of the scholarship of the time.

29 There are works which explicitly suggest that Sufism is not Islam or Sufism is different from Islam, although it sometimes finds a place in Islam. See: Elwell Sutton, "Sufism and Pseudo-Sufism, *Islam in the Modern World*", Ed. Denis MacEoin and Ahmad Al-Shahi (New York: St. Martin's, 1983), 49-56. Some of the most interesting examples on this issue are the works of Annemarie Schimmel. Although she expresses that Sufism is a dimension of Islam, as is obvious in her book titled *Mystical Dimensions of Islam*, one can find the ideas in her books stating just the opposite: see *Mystical Dimensions of Islam*, p. 131, p. 180, p. 342. Abdülbaki Gölpınarlı is another example. He presents Sufism as a movement that is separated from and working against Islam. See his *Melamiler ve Melamilik* (Istanbul: Gri, 1992), introduction, p. 26 and p. 90. Seyyed Hos-

sein Nasr, William Chittick and Martin Lings can be counted among the scholars who argue that Sufism is an inherent part of Islam.

30 Nawawi, *An Nawawi's Forty Hadith,* translated by Ezzeddin Ibrahim and Danys Johnson Davis, 3rd edition (Lahore: Ahbab, 1979). The hadith is also found in many classical hadith collections, such as Bukhari and Muslim. Due to the importance of this hadith the whole text is quoted here. Umar ibn al-Khattab reports: "One day while we were sitting with the Messenger of God there appeared before us a man whose clothes were exceedingly white and whose hair was exceedingly black; no signs of travel were to be seen on him and none of us knew him. He walked up and sat down by the Prophet. Resting his knees against the Prophet's and placing the palms of his hands on his thighs, he said: "O Muhammad, tell me about Islam." The Messenger of God said: "Islam is to testify that there is no deity but God and Muhammad is the Messenger of God, to perform the prayers, to pay the *zakah*, to fast in Ramadan, and to make the pilgrimage to the House [of God in Mecca] if you are able to do so." He said: "You have spoken rightly," and we were amazed at him asking the Prophet and saying that he had spoken rightly. He said: "Then tell me about *iman*." He said: "It is to believe in God, His angels, His Books, His Prophets, and the Last Day, and to believe in divine destiny, both the good and the evil thereof." He said: "You have spoken rightly." He said: "Then tell me about *ihsan.*" He said: "It is to worship God as though you were seeing Him, for even if you do not see Him, He sees you." He said: "Then tell me about the Hour." He said: "The one questioned about it knows no better than the questioner." He said: "Then tell me about its signs." He said: "That the slave-girl will give birth to her mistress and that you will see the barefooted, naked, destitute herdsman competing in constructing lofty buildings." Then he took himself off and I stayed for a time. Then he said: "O Umar, do you know who the questioner was?" I said: "God and His Messenger know best." He said: "He was Gabriel, who came to you to teach you your religion."

31 Luis Massignon, *Essays on the Origin of the Technical Language of Islamic Mysticism.* Translated from the French with an introduction by Benjamin Clark. Foreword by Herbert Mason. (Notre Dame, Indiana: University of Notre Dame Press, 1997), p. 132.

32 Hadith qudsi are divine words transmitted through Prophet Muhammad which are separate from Qur'anic verses.

33 This type of hadith is not transmitted verbally but by way of unveiling (*kashf*). See: William C. Chittick, *The Sufi Path of Knowledge,* (Albany: State University of New York Press, 1989), p. 391.

34 Sheikh Galib (1757-1799) expresses this idea in a beautiful couplet: *Hoşça bak zatına kim zübde-i alemsin sen / Merdüm-i dide-i ekvan olan ademsin sen*. ("Look at yourself with careful attention, since you are the essence of the universe, You are a human being who is the pupil of the eye of the universe") Abdülbaki Gölpınarlı, *Şeyh Galip* (Istanbul: Varlık, 1953), p. 38.

35 See Abd al-Karim ibn Hawazin Qushayri, *Sufi Book of Spiritual Ascent (al-Risala al-Qushayriya),* translated by Rabia Harris, edited by Laleh Bakhtiar (Chicago, IL: ABC Group International, 1997); Annemarie Schimmel, *Mystical Dimensions of Islam,* pp. 107–127.

36 Yunus Emre also presents the same scene in one of his poems: *Yunus Emre Divanı*, II, p. 24.

37 Chittick, *The Sufi Path of Knowledge*, p. 325.

38 Marshall G. S. Hodgson, *Venture of Islam, Conscience and History in World Civilization,* 3 vols. (Chicago: University of Chicago Press, 1974), Vol. I, p. 393.

39 Margaret Smith, *The Life and Work of Rabia and Other Women Mystics in Islam* (Oxford: Oneworld, 1994).

40 Only small portions of this work have been translated into English: Abu Halid Muhammad ibn Muhammad, Ghazali, *Al-Ghazali on the Manners Relating to Eating: Book XI of the Revival of the Religious Sciences; Kitab Adab al-Akl; Ihya-yi Ulum al-Din,* by Denys Johnson Davies (Cambridge: Islamic Texts Society, 2000).

41 Gölpınarlı, *Yunus Emre ve Tasavvuf,* pp. 234-235.

42 Başgöz, I, p. 133.

43 Faruk Kadri Timurtaş, *Yunus Emre Divanı* (Istanbul: Tercüman, 1972), p. 25.

44 Ahmet Kabaklı, *Türk Edebiyatı*, (Istanbul: Türkiye Yayınları, 1968), p. 157.

45 Sezai Karakoç, *Yunus Emre* (Istanbul: Diriliş, 1965), p. 11.

46 *Menakıb-i Hacı Bektaş-ı Veli "Vilayetname,"* (ed.) Abdülbaki Gölpınarlı (Istanbul: İnkılap, 1958); *Firdevs-i Rumi Manzum Hacı Bektaş Vilayetnamesi,* (ed.) Bedri Noyan (Istanbul: Can, 1996); Hacı Bektaş-ı Veli, *Makalat,* (ed.) Esad Coşan (Istanbul: Seha, 1982).

47 Alevi [or 'Alawi]: of or pertaining to 'Ali, the cousin and son-in-law of the Prophet.

48 Gölpınarlı, *Yunus Emre ve Tasavvuf,* p. 234. All of these could also be found in Birge's *Bektashi Order of Dervishes.*

49 Ibid., p. 234.

50 Ibid., p. 235.

51 See Recep Bilginer, *Yunus Emre* (Istanbul: Cem, 1979); Gönül Alpay, "Yunus Emre'nin Humanizmasının Temelleri," in *Uluslararası Yunus Emre Semineri, Istanbul 6-7-8 September 1971* (Istanbul: Baha, 1971); İsmet Zeki Eyuboğlu, *Yunus Emre, Bir Ozanın İç Evreninde Gezintiler* (Istanbul: Geçit, 1991); Abdullah Rıza Ergüven, *Bütün Yönleriyle Yunus Emre* (Istanbul: Bergin, 2001).

52 Irene Melikoff, "Yunus Emre ve Bektaşilik," in *Uluslararası Yunus Emre Semineri,* ("International Yunus Emre Seminar"), Istanbul, 6–8 September 1971 (Istanbul: Baha, 1971), p. 298.

53 *Menakıb-ı Hacı Bektaş-ı Veli,* 1.; *Firdevs-i Rumi Manzum Hacı Bektaş Vilayetnamesi* by Bedri Noyan (Istanbul: Can, 1996), p. 108.

54 *Menakıb-ı Hacı Bektaş-ı Veli,* p. 99.

55 Ibid., p. 41.

56 Ibid., p. 45.

57 Ibid., p. 49.

58 Anna Masala, "Adı Güzel Kendi Güzel Muhammed," in *IV. Uluslararası Halk Edebiyatı ve Yunus Emre Semineri* (Fourth International Folk Literature and Yunus Emre Conference), 11–13 May 1989, (Eskişehir: Eskişehir Valiliği Yayınları, 1991), p. 257.

59 Yunus Emre, II, p. 147.

60 Ibid., II, pp. 102, 146, 246, 270, 321, 343 and 349.

61 Yunus Emre, II, p. 142.

62 Gölpınarlı (ed.), *Vilayetname*, p.76.

63 Noyan, Bedri, *Bütün Yönleriyle Bektaşilik ve Alevilik,* (Ankara: Ardıç Yay., 1988), v.1, p. 446.

64 See the section on "the Reception of Yunus Emre in the Ottoman Period" in Chapter 3.

65 Birge calls Shah Ismail one of the most influential propagators of Shiite thought in Anatolia. Birge, *Bektashi Order of Dervishes*, p. 68. See the section on the reception of Yunus Emre in the Ottoman Period.

66 Birge, *Bektashi Order of Dervishes,* pp. 69–70, F.W. Hasluck, *Christianity and Islam Under the Sultans,* 2 vols. (Oxford: Clerendon Press, 1929), v.1, pp. 138–166.

67 V. Minorski, "the Poetry of Shah Ismail I", *Bulletin of the School of Oriental and African Studies, University of London*, v.10, issue 4, 1942, pp. 1006a–1053.

68 "Ben yanarım dünü günü, Bana Seni gerek Seni" ["I burn day and night / What I need is You, You"] and Shah Ismail "Bana Ali gerek Ali" ["What I need is Ali, Ali"], Gölpınarlı, *Yunus Emre ve Tasavvuf,* p. 239.

69 Yakup Kadri Karaosmanoğlu, *Nur Baba* (Istanbul: Akşam, 1922). Although it is likely that this book ranks in the lower end of the literary works of the author, the fact that this book has been translated into German and Spanish is significant in terms of showing the criteria for translation.

70 Schimmel, *Mystical Dimensions of Islam,* p. 156; Birge, *Bektashi Order of Dervishes,* p. 20.

71 Gölpınarlı (ed.), *Vilayetname*, p. 5.

72 Gölpınarlı, *Melamilik ve Melamiler*, pp. iii-iv.

73 Ahmet Yaşar Ocak, *Osmanlı İmparatorluğunda Marjinal Sufilik: Kalenderiler* (Ankara: Türk Tarih Kurumu Basımevi, 1992), pp. 69–75. See also Gölpınarlı, *Yunus Emre ve Tasavvuf,* pp. 21, 23.

74 Ahmet Yaşar Ocak argues that Yunus Emre was a Malami-Qalandari dervish. See Ocak, *Osmanlı İmparatorluğunda Marjinal Sufilik,* p. 67.

75 *Redhouse Yeni Türkçe İngilizce Sözlük* (Istanbul: Redhouse, 1968), p. 750.

76 Gölpınarlı, *Melamilik ve Melamiler* and by the same author *Yüz Soruda Türkiye'de Mezhepler ve Tarikatlar Tarihi* (Istanbul: Gerçek Yayınevi, 1969) pp. 246–247.

77 Seyyed Hossein Nasr's preface to *Fakhruddin Iraqi: Divine Flashes,* p. 4.

78 Gölpınarlı, *Melamilik ve Melamiler,* pp. 14–15.

79 The verse is "*O you who believe! If any from among you turn back from his Faith, soon will God produce, a people whom He loves, and who love Him, most humble towards the believers, dignified and commanding in the face of the unbelievers, fighting in the way of God, and never afraid of the reproaches.*" (Qur'an 5:54)

80 Chittick, *The Sufi Path of Knowledge*, p. 373.

81 Ibid., pp. 372-374.

82 "*Travel through the earth and see what was the end of those who rejected Truth.*" (6:11); "*Do they not travel though the land so that their hearts (and minds) may thus learn wisdom.*" (22:46) and also (27:69), (29:20–22), (30:9, 42) and (35:44).

83 Eric Auerbach, *Mimesis, the Representation of Reality in Western Literature* (New York: Doubleday and Anchor, 1957), p. 492.

84 Terry Eagleton, *Literary Theory, an Introduction (*Oxford: Blackwell, 1983), p. 22.

85 *Ulusal Karşılaştırmalı Edebiyat Semposyumu, 06–08 December 2001* (Eskişehir: Osman Gazi University, 2002).

86 Susan Bassnett, *Comparative Literature, a Critical Introduction* (Oxford UK, Cambridge USA: Blackwell, 1993), p. 14.

87 Ibid., pp. 15–16.

88 Ahmet Yaşar Ocak, *Türk Sufiliğine Bakışlar*, p. 128.

89 Annemarie Schimmel, *The Triumphal Sun, a Study of the Works of Jalaluddin Rumi* (London: Fine Book, 1978), p. 333.

90 Ibid., p. 334.

91 Rumi, quoted in Schimmel, *The Triumphal Sun,* p. 335.

92 Halman, *Yunus Emre and His Mystical Poetry,* p. 164.

93 Schimmel, *The Triumphal Sun,* p. 336.

94 There is the reference here to the "*maratib al-wujud*" (the chain of being) from minerals to plants and animals.

95 Rumi, quoted in Annemarie Schimmel, *The Triumphal Sun,* p. 328.

96 The poetry of Fuzuli is a prime example of this idea. His "*Aşk derdiyle hoşem el çek ilacımdan tabip/Kılma derman kim helakim zehri dermanumdadır*" ("I am content with the sickness of love, do not prescribe me any medication, o doctor / Do not cure me, as your cure will be my destruction") is a good summary of this understanding. Tarlan, Ali Nihad, *Fuzuli Divanı Şerhi* (Ankara: Kültür ve Turizm Bakanlığı Yay, 1985), vol.1, p. 304.

97 Rumi, quoted in Schimmel, *The Triumphal Sun,* p. 348.

98 Yunus Emre Divanı, II, p. 102, p. 146, p. 246, p. 270, p. 321, p. 343 and p. 349.

99 Eflaki, *Menakib al-Arifin,* Ed. Tahsin Yazıcı (Ankara, 1959), p. 201, p. 227, p. 350, p. 395, p. 406 and p. 441.

100 Rumi, quoted in Schimmel, *The Triumphal Sun,* p. 303.

101 Ibid., p. 290.

102 Ibid.

103 Qur'an 96:19.

104 Schimmel, *The Triumphal Sun*, p. 356.

105 Annemarie Schimmel states "...Rumi's stories are without beginning and end. He often starts with one tale, then is carried away by a loose association of words or thought, and may insert a second, even [a] third story, until he reminds himself to return once more to the basic anecdote." And she concludes, "This looseness of the *Mathnawi*, which most Western readers find difficult to appreciate is reminiscent of the form of a mystical session." Schimmel, *The Triumphal Sun,* p. 50. This style also has another aspect: Not only is it reminiscent of a Sufi mystical session, it also brings to mind the Qur'an. The stories told in the *Mathnawi* are mostly already known in that environment. Rumi is using these stories just as a pretext, to get attention or to make the topic he is expressing more lively and accessible.

106 Franklin Lewis, *Rumi: Past and Present, East and West: the Life and Teaching and Poetry of Jalal al Din Rumi* (Oxford, Boston: Oneworld, 2000), p. 313.

107 Lewis, p. 314.

108 Schimmel, *The Triumphal Sun,* p. 42.

109 Rumi, quoted in Schimmel, *The Triumphal Sun,* p. 43.

Chapter 2: An Analysis of Yunus Emre's Poetry

1 In the case of Rumi, Schimmel discusses the famous Qur'anic verse which says, "*And they say what they themselves do not do*" (26:226) in reference to poets, and asserts that "...For many pious Muslims, [poetry] was something almost immoral." See Schimmel, *I am Wind You are Fire,* p. 34. There is no historic evidence for this statement and Turkish Sufi history alone can produce hundreds of counter examples to refute it. This statement is an extension of the division that we observe in some other works of Schimmel and many other Orientalists, which is a division between Islam and Sufism or the pious Muslim and the Sufi.

2 Köprülü, *Türk Edebiyatında İlk Mutasavvıflar,* p. 295.

3 Ibid., p. 300.

4 There are many poems of Yunus Emre which could be categorized as didactic poetry; in these, the main priority seems to be to give advice and disseminate teachings. See: Yunus Emre, I, p. 173, p. 237, p. 239, p. 251, p. 293, p. 306, p. 329, p. 332.

5 Toprak, pp. 30-34.

6 Yunus Emre, II, p. 94.

7 Ibid., p. 22.

8 Ahmet Yaşar Ocak, *Türk Sufiliğine Bakışlar,* p. 39.

9 There are few poems that could be considered in this category, as Schimmel points out. Schimmel, *Mystical Dimensions of Islam,* p. 333.

10 Edited version of Halman' s translation. Halman, *Mystical Poetry of Yunus Emre,* p. 149.

11 Based on this poem one interpreter, Sebahattin Eyüboğlu, asserts that "Yunus rebels against God, he doubts His justice, and in this way he criticizes God." Sebahattin Eyüboğlu, p. 38.

12 *Encyclopedia of Islam* (Leiden: Brill, 1954), p. 366.

13 Ibid., p. 369.

14 Ibid.

15 There are various editions of this work. See Mustafa Tatçı, *Risaletü'n Nushiyye* (Ankara: Kültür Bakanlığı, 1991); Umay Günay and Osman Horata, *Risaletü'n Nushiyye* (Ankara: Diyanet, 1994).

16 Walter G. Andrews defines *yekahenk* as "[poems] which one can say clearly are about something; that is about the Prophet, about God, about the bath etc." Walter G. Andrew, *An Introduction to Ottoman Poetry* (Minneapolis: Bibliotheca Islamica, 1976, p. 140).

17 There are 415 poems in the most comprehensive and scholarly edition of Yunus Emre's *Divan*. *Yunus Emre,* 2 vols. Ed. Mustafa Tatçı (Ankara: Kültür Bakanlığı, 1990).

18 Yunus Emre, II, p. 198.

19 Recep Bilginer, *Yunus Emre* (Istanbul: Cem, 1979).

20 Hasan Kıyafet, *Ölülerle Söyleşi* (Ankara: Doruk, 1995).

21 Sebahattin Eyüboğlu, *Yunus Emre* (Istanbul: Cem, 1980).

22 Yunus Emre, II, p. 78, p. 233, p. 388.

23 Sezai Karakoç, for instance, classifies the poetry of Yunus Emre as lyrical poems about nature, metaphysical poems about death, and poems about the foundations of Islam. (Karakoç, p. 37).

24 Schimmel, *Mystical Dimensions of Islam,* p. 333.

25 The fact that the poems of Yunus Emre were used in many different *tariqas* and were accepted in the modern period by very diverse groups is an indication of this.

26 Makaryk, Irena R. (ed), *Encyclopedia of Contemporary Literary Theory: Approaches, Scholars, and Terms*, (Toronto: University of Toronto Press, 1995), p. 120.

27 Ibid., p. 125.

28 Ibid., p. 122.

29 See Appendix I for the original of the poem.

30 This is not a hadith transmitted from the Prophet, but it is accepted as being authentic by many Sufis on the bases of unveiling *(kashf)*. For a brief discussion of the issue, see: Chittick, *Sufi Path of Knowledge,* pp. 250–252.

31 Chittick, *Sufi Path of Knowledge,* p. 396.

32 Izutsu, Toshihiko, *A Comparative Study of the Key Philosophical Concepts In Sufism and Taoism, Ibn Arabi and Lao Tzu, Chuang-Tzu* (Tokyo: Keio University, 1966), p. 238.

33 Ibid., p. 200.

34 Ibid., p. 213.

35 Fazlurrahman, *Islam*, 2nd edition (Chicago: University of Chicago Press, 1979), p. 146.

36 Qur'an, 2:215.

37 *Ibn Ataillah's Sufi Aphorisms (Kitab al-Hikam)*, Translated with an introduction and notes by Victor Danner, foreword by Martin Lings (Leiden: E.J.Brill, 1973, p. 78).

38 Chittick, *Sufi Path of Knowledge,* p. 139.

39 Hakim, Suad, *al-Mujam as-Sufi* (Beirut: Dandara, 1981), 1261. Quoted in William C. Chittick, *Sufi Path of Love, The Spiritual Teachings of Rumi* (Albany: SUNY, 1983), p. 107.

40 Chittick, *Sufi Path of Love,* p. 112.

41 Ibid., *Sufi Path of Knowledge*, p. 345.

42 Ibid., p. 344.

43 Schimmel, *I am Wind You are Fire,* pp. 167-168.

44 Alessio Bombaci, trans. Kathleen R. F. Griffin-Burrill, ed. Uli Schamiloglu, *The Literature of the Turks* (Madison: Turko-Tatar Press, forthcoming), pp. 263-283.

45 Melikoff, *Efsaneden Gerçeğe*, p. 281.

46 İsmet Zeki Eyüboğlu, p. 118. Eyüboğlu provides a poem and argues that there are fifty-three words in the poem and only three of them are foreign, i.e. Arabic or Persian.

47 Ibid., p. 114.

48 Said Khourshid, *La langue de Yunus Emre Contribution A L'Hitoire du Turc pre-Ottoman* (Ankara: Editions Ministere de La Culture, 1991), pp. 61-64; Abdurrahman Güzel also provides a similar ratio for the linguistic origin of the words in the poetry of Yunus Emre. Abdurrahman Güzel, *Mutasavvıf Yunus Emre* (Ankara: Kılıç, 1991), p. 51.

49 İsmet Zeki Eyüboğlu, p. 21.

50 Halman, p. 13.

51 Karakoç, p. 44.

52 *Encyclopedia of Contemporary Literary Theory*, s.v. "Chomsky."

53 Fish, Stanley, *Is There a Text in This Class: the Authority of Interpretive Communities*, (London and Massachusetts: Cambridge and Harvard Universities, 1980), p. 97.

54 Roland Barthes, *Image, Music, Text*, Essays Selected and Translated by Stephen Heath, (London: Fortana, 1977), p. 146.

55 Many scholars, such as E. J. W. Gibb and John Walsh, agree that Yunus Emre was part of the larger Muslim Sufi culture and did not introduce a new philosophy. Gibb says, "all the philosophy of Yunus will be found in the *Divan* of Jelal." (Elias John Wilkinson Gibb, A History of Ottoman Poetry, 6 vols. (London: Luzac, 1958), v.1, p. 169; Walsh, p. 124.

56 İsmet Zeki Eyüboğlu, p. 49.

57 Ibid., p. 57.

58 For a discussion of the reason why Yunus Emre composed poetry, see Toprak, v.2, p. 30-34.

59 Gölpınarlı states that "he presented the poems in a language that is as close as possible to the language spoken today." Gölpınarlı, *Yunus Emre ve Tasavvuf,* p. 369.

Chapter 3: Reception of Yunus Emre

1 Namık Kemal, *Talim-i Edebiyata Dair Risale,* ("Pamphlet on Literary Education") in *Ondokuzuncu Asır Türk Edebiyatı Tarihi* by Ahmet Hamdi Tanpınar (Istanbul: Çağlayan, 1988), p. 344.

2 T. S. Eliot, "Tradition and Indivudual Talent," in *Criticism, Major Statements,* Selected and edited by Charles Kaplan and William Anderson, 3rd ed., p. 433.

3 David Bleich, *Readings and Feelings: An Introduction to Subjective Criticism* (Urbana, Ill.: National Council of Teachers of English 1975), p. 68.

4 Hans Robert Jauss, *Toward an Aesthetic Reception*, (translation from German by Timothy Bahti), Introduction by Paul de Man (New York: St. Martin's Press, 1982), pp. 21–22.

5 Fish, p. 171.

6 Wolfgang Iser, *The Act of Reading: a theory of aesthetic response* (Baltimore: Johns Hopkins University Press, 1971), p. 54.

7 Wolfgang Iser, *Prospecting: from reader response to literary anthropology* (Baltimore: Johns Hopkins, 1989), p. 203.

8 Hans Robert Jauss, *Aesthetic Experience and Literary Hermeneutics, Asthetische Erfahrung und Literarische Hermeneutik* (Minneapolis: University of Minnesota Press, 1982), p. 167.

9 Ahmet Kabaklı, *Yunus Emre* (Istanbul: Türk Edebiyatı Vakfı, 1991), p. 13.

10 We should also mention the problem of the script for the poetry of Yunus Emre. In contemporary Turkey, only a handful of experts are able to read the Ottoman script. The book by Orhan Şaik Gökyay makes fun of misreading the Ottoman script. Orhan Şaik Gökyay, *Destursuz Bağa Girenler* (Istanbul: Dergah, 1982).

11 Ahmet Yaşar Ocak, Mustafa Tahralı, Annemarie Schimmel, and Grace Martin Smith are among the scholars who consider Yunus Emre within the Sufi tradition.

12 For the opinion of Ali Emiri Efendi see *Tarih ve Edebiyat Mecmuası*, year 3, no: 25-31 March, 1336, p. 635.

13 Abdülbaki Gölpınarlı, *Tasavvuftan Dilimize Geçen Deyimler ve Atasözleri* ("Idioms and Proverbs Originating from Sufism in Turkish Language"), (Istanbul: İnkılap ve Aka, 1977).

14 Ferdinand de Saussure, *Course in General Linguistics;* edited by Charles Bally and Albert Sechehaye in collaboration with Albert Riedlinger; translated, with an introduction and notes, by Wade Baskin (New York: McGraw-Hill Book Co., 1966).

15 Nobody has attempted to analyze the Turkish Language Revolution in terms of the outcome of linguistic theories, since it is still a political issue. The theory of Ferdinand de Saussure, who is the founder of modern linguistics, would be a useful analytical tool for this purpose.

16 I have used Fuat Köprülü's *Türk Edebiyatında İlk Mutasavvıflar* ("The First Mystics in Turkish Literature") and Abdulkadir Gölpınarlı's *Yunus Emre ve Tasavvuf* ("Yunus Emre and Sufism") as my primary sources. Fuat Köprülü, *Türk Edebiyatında İlk Mutasavvıflar* ("The First Mystics in Turkish Literature"), (Ankara: Türk Tarih Kurumu, 1976). [First edition in 1919]; Abdülbaki Gölpınarlı, *Yunus Emre ve Tasavvuf* ("Yunus Emre and Sufism"), (Istanbul: Remzi, 1961*)*.

17 The text of *Vilayetname* was written in the 15th century by a disciple of Hacı Bektaş, Uzun Firdevsi. For a discussion of this person, see: Firdevsi, *Kutbname*, eds: I. Olgun and I. Parmaksızoğlu (Ankara: Türk Tarih Kurumu Yayınları, 1980). *Vilayetname* is important in terms of showing the image / reception of Yunus Emre in Bektashi tradition. There are two modern editions of the book: *Velayet-i Hacı Bektaşi Veli*, Abdülbaki Gölpınarlı (ed.), Istanbul: İnkılab, 1990. *Hacı Bektaş Veli Manzum Vilayetnamesi.* Bedri Noyan (ed.), (Istanbul: Can, 1996).

18 Ziver Tezeren, *Seyyid Aziz Mahmud Hüdai, Hayatı Şahsiyeti,Tarikatı ve Eserleri* (Istanbul: Edebiyat Fakültesi, 1984).

19 Aşık Çelebi, *Meşairü'ş-Şuara*, Faximile edition, G.M. Meredith Oweno, 1971, p. 98b.

20 Ali Yılmaz, *Şeyhi Süleyman Efendi*, (Ankara: Kültür Bakanlığı, 1989).

21 Gölpınarlı, *Yunus Emre ve Tasavvuf,* p. 58.

22 What I mean by "the information in oral sources" is the information that is not found in any of the works written in the Ottoman period. I have used two sources substantially. The first one is by Çağatay Uluçay. *Yunus Emre'nin Mezarı*, Istanbul: Remzi, 1943 and the second one is by Abdülbaki Gölpınarlı. *Yunus Emre ve Tasavvuf* ("Yunus Emre and Sufism"), (Istanbul: Remzi, 1961) although these accounts can be found in many other collections.

23 Gölpınarlı, *Yunus Emre ve Tasavvuf,* p. 66.

24 Gölpınarlı (ed.), *Vilayetname* (Istanbul: Can, 1990), Introduction.

25 *Firdevs-i Rumi, Manzum Hacı Bektaşı Veli Rivayetnamesi,* p. 12.

26 Ibid., p. 14.

27 Ahmet Yaşar Ocak, *Kültür Tarihi Kaynağı Olarak Menakıbnameler: Metodolojik Bir Yaklaşım*, (Ankara: Türk Tarih Kurumu, 1992).

28 Hacı Bektaş Veli, *Manzum Velayetnamesi,* Bedri Noyan (ed.), (Istanbul: Can, 1996), p. 27.

29 See Cem Dilçin, *Nazire* in *Örneklerle Şiir Bilgisi* (Ankara: Türk Dil Kurumu, 1995), [1st edition 1983], pp. 269-273. *Nazire* in *An Introduction to Ottoman Poetry* by Walter G. Andrews. (Minneapolis: Bibliotheca Islamica, 1976), pp. 165–166. The best treatment of *nazira* is in *On Dokuzuncu Asır Türk Edebiyatı Tarihi* by Ahmet Hamdi Tanpinar (Istanbul: Çağlayan, 7th edition, 1988), pp. 20–22.

30 Gölpınarlı gives these poems in his *Yunus Emre ve Tasavvuf,* p. 206.

31 See Appendix II for the original of the poem.

32 See Appendix III for the original of the poem.

33 Eşrefoğlu Rumi, *Eşrefoğlu Rumi Divanı, İnceleme, Karşılaştırmalı Metin,* Mustafa Güneş (ed.), (Ankara: Dumlupınar Üniversitesi Yayınları, 2000).

34 Himmet Konur, *İbrahim Gülşeni Hayatı Eserleri Tarikatı* (Istanbul: İnsan, 2002).

35 Sadettin Nuzhet Ergün, *Hatayi Divanı, Şah İsmail Safevi: Edebi Hayatı ve Nefesleri* (İstanbul: Maarif, 1959); Victor Minorski, The Poetry of Shah İsmail I, *Bulletin of the School of Oriental Studies,* University of London, vol.10, issue: 4, (1942), pp. 1006a-1053a.

36 See appendix IV for the original of the poem.

37 See appendix V for the original of the poem.

38 Gölpınarlı, *Yunus Emre ve Tasavvuf*, p. 220.

39 Yunus Emre, II, p. 167.

40 Üftade, *Divan-ı Hazret-i Üftade*, Bursalı Mehmet Tahir (ed.), (Istanbul: Necm-i İstiklal Matbaası, 1912).

41 Gölpınarlı, *Yunus Emre ve Tasavvuf,* p. 222.

42 Gölpınarlı, *Yunus Emre ve Tasavvuf,* pp. 224–225.

43 Derin Terzioğlu, *Sufi and Dissent in the Ottoman Empire, Niyazi Mısri 1618–1694*, Doctoral dissertation (Harvard University, 1999); Kenan Erdoğan, *Niyazi Mısri Niyazi-i Mısri: Hayatı, Edebi Kişiliği, Eserleri ve Divanı: Tenkitli metin* (Ankara: Akçağ, 1998).

44 This poem starts with "I climbed on a branch of plum tree and ate grape up there." (Gölpınarlı, *Yunus Emre ve Tasavvuf,* p. 230).

45 There are various editions containing this account. I used *Yunus Emre'nin Şahsiyeti ve Yunus Emre Şerhleri, Yunus Emre'nin Bir Eserinin Şerhleriyle İlgili Yazmaları,* by Necla Pekolcay and Emine Sevim (Ankara: Kültür Bakanlığı Yayınları, 1991), pp. 139–140.

46 *Tarihi ve Kültürel Boyutlarıyla Türkiyede Aleviler, Bektaşiler, Nusayriler* ("Alevites, Bektashis and Nusayris in Turkey with Historical and Cultural Dimensions"), (Conference volume) (Istanbul: Ensar Neşriyat, 1999).

47 Hüseyin Kazım Kadri, *Büyük Türk Lugati*, ("Extensive Turkish Dictionary") (Istanbul: Remzi, 1943), pp. 217–218.

48 There are other commentaries on the works of Yunus Emre. However, since there is debate about whether these poems belong to Yunus Emre and since these commentaries are not significantly different from what I have discussed here, I will not include them into my discussion. See Ömür Ceylan, *Tasavvufi Şiir Şerhleri* ("The Commentaries on Mystical Poems"), (Istanbul: Kitabevi, 2000), pp. 43–44.

49 These commentaries can be found in many libraries as manuscripts; they have also been printed in many books. I have used the texts published by A. Necla Pekolcay and Emine Sevim in *Yunus Emrenin Şahsiyeti ve Yunus Emre Şerhleri, Yunus Emre'nin Bir Eseriyle İlgili Şerhlerinin Yazmaları* ("The Personality of Yunus Emre and the commentaries on Yunus Emre, The Manuscripts of the Commentary of a Work of Yunus Emre"), (Ankara: Kültür Bakanlığı, 1991).

50 Pekolcay, p. 77.

51 Ibid., p. 176, p. 183.

52 Ibid., p. 85.

53 Ibid., p. 85.

54 Ibid., p. 87.

55 Ibid., p. 136.

56 Ibid., p. 78.

57 Ibid., p. 78.

58 Ibid., p. 79.

59 Ibid., p. 86.

60 Ibid., p. 176.

61 Ibid., pp. 97–125.

62 In the four commentaries discussed here, there are about 45 Qur'anic verses and 35 hadiths; only a few of them have a Turkish explanation. See Pekolcay, pp. 209–218.

63 Hoca Saadettin, *Tacü't-Tevarih,* İsmet Parmaksızoğlu (ed.), (Ankara: Kültür Bakanlığı, 1992).

64 Pekolcay, p. 178.

65 "ve ol Hazreti zat…varlık alemini bana ayan edip açtı ve gösterdi ve ben dahi seyr edip gördüğümden sonra nagah Hazreti Yunus Emre'nin yedi beyit bir muğlak gazeli gözüme tuş olup… mana-yı latifelerin bu yedi beyit gazel-i garranın içinden Hak teala celle ve ala bana bir bir ayan edip bildürdi ve gösterdi." Pekolcay, pp. 77–78.

66 Niyazi Mısri says "one night I saw Yunus," without specifying whether in a dream or in a vision. One interpreter takes up this issue and discusses whether Niyazi Misri saw Yunus in his dream or as a *yakaza*, a special condition between sleep and waking. Talip Hafızoğlu, *Çıktım Erik Dalına* (İzmir: Çağlayan,

1981), p. 81. For more information on this issue see: John J. Lamoreaux, *The Early Muslim Tradition of Dream Interpretation*, (Albany: SUNY, 2002).

67 Dreams and interpretations of the dreams were an important part of acquiring knowledge in Sufism and in Islamic culture. Dreams are even considered to be a channel for Divine illuminations and inspirations. See: *Türk Edebiyatında Tasavvufi Rüya Tabirleri* ("Mystical Dream Interpretations in Turkish Literature"), by Mustafa Tatçı and Halil Çeltik, (Ankara: Akçağ, 1995).

68 "*Bir gice Yunus Emre hazretlerini gördüm. Bu fakire azim beşaşet ile iltifat gösterip söyledi ki' benüm ol sözlerime yazdığın şerhi ve didüğin meani-i latifi fukaradan ve talibinden diriğ etme, vir menfaatlensünler' diyü fakire tenbih buyurdular. Ve bu fakire didi ki: 'Benüm ol iplik virdüm çulhaya beytine yazduğun manayı yazma. İşte şu manayı yaz' diye yazıcak sözi beyan buyurdılar. Zira bu beyte bir ahar mana yazmış idim andan fariğ olunup bu manada yazıldı felehu.*" Pekolcay, pp. 144–145.

69 Pekolcay, p. 113.

70 Ibid., p. 55.

71 Ibid., p. 175.

72 Ibid., p. 72.

73 Ibid., p. 184.

74 Ibid., p. 176.

75 Ibid., pp. 167, 179, 181.

76 Ibid., p. 113.

77 An interesting discussion on this issue can be found in *The Unreadable Shores of Love, Turkish Modernity and Mystic Romance* by Victoria Rove Holbrook (Austin: University of Austin Press, 1994), p. 130.

78 Gölpınarlı, *Melamilik and Melamiler,* Introduction.

79 Pekolcay, p. 184. This is the famous *Ihya al-Ulumi'd-Din* ("Revival of Religious Sciences") by al-Ghazali.

80 Cem Behar, a Turkish musicologist, has an interesting theory regarding the role of improvisation. According to him, writing down the compositions with musical notes cemented the performance and prevented different individuals from creating their own personal interpretation for the same composition, and thus was not a common practice. Cem Behar, *Türk Musikisi Üzerine Denemeler* (Istanbul: Bağlam, 1987).

81 An *aşık* [or *ashik*] is a mystic troubadour or traveling bard who sings and plays the *saz*, a form of lute.

82 Rauf Yekta, *İlahiler: Mevlüt Tevsihleri,* v.1, Istanbul, in Walter Feldman, "Didactism and Authority in the Liturgical Poetry of the Halveti Dervishes of Istanbul," *Edebiyat,* V.NS4, p. 254.

83 Rüştü Sardağ, *Buhurizade Mustafa Itri Efendi* (Ankara: Kültür Bakanlığı, 1989).

84 Yahya Kemal Beyatlı, *Kendi Gök Kubbemiz* (Istanbul: Istanbul Fetih Cemiyeti, 1997), p. 17.

85 Gölpınarlı, *Yunus Emre ve Tasavvuf*, p. 248.

86 Süleymaniye Library. Esad Efendi Kitapları. Manuscript no: 3397, quoted in Gölpınarlı, *Yunus Emre ve Tasavvuf*, p. 247.

87 Cemalettin Revnakoğlu, How and Where were the Hymns of Yunus Emre Chanted? In *Yunus Emre, The Great Turkish Mystic* (Ankara: Kültür Bakanlığı, 1991), pp. 108–132.

88 Gölpınarlı, *Yunus Emre ve Tasavvuf*, p. 248.

89 Walter Feldman, "Didactism and Authority in the Liturgical Poetry of the Halveti Dervishes of Istanbul," pp. 243–264.

90 Fuat Köprülü asserts that the influence of Yunus Emre on *ashik* literature was indirect, mentioning the Bektashi ties with the Janissaries and their influence on *ashik* literature. *Türk Edebiyatında İlk Mutasavvıflar* ("First Mystics in Turkish Literature"), p. 355. Ergün quotes from *Vakıat-ı Üftade* written by the disciples of Şeyh Üftade (d.1580–1581).

91 Revnakoğlu, p. 112.

92 Sadettin Nuzhet Ergün, *Türk Musikisi Antolojisi,* ("Anthology of Turkish Music"), (Istanbul: Rıza Koşgun Matbaası, 1942), p. 8.

93 Taha Parla, *The Social and Political Thought of Ziya Gökalp* (Leiden: E. J. Brill, 1985).

94 Ali Nihat Tarlan, *Mehmet Akif, His Life and Works* (Ankara: Ministry of Culture and Tourism, 1986).

95 Mehmet Kaplan, *Tevfik Fikret, Devir Şahsiyet Eser* (Istanbul, 1971).

96 Uriel Heid, *Foundations of Turkish Nationalism, The Life and Teaching of Ziya Gökal*p (London: Luzac, 1950).

97 Köprülü, *Demokrasi Yolunda* (The Hauge: Mouton, 1964).

98 Gökalp, p. 24.

99 Köprülü, *Türk Edebiyatında İlk Mutasavvıflar* ("The First Mystics in Turkish Literature"), p. 1.

100 Ibid.

101 The first person, who is referred to as Mulbahlı [of Mulbah] as his name is unknown, to translate the poems of Yunus Emre into a Western language was a prisoner of war captured by the Ottomans in 1438 who lived in Turkey for 20 years. When he left the country, he brought back two poems of Yunus Emre copied in Gothic letters and translated them into Latin. This is a significant piece of information demonstrating the popularity of the poetry of Yunus Emre at the time. Yunus Emre, II, p. 39.

102 Gibb, p. 6.

103 Ibid., p. 7.

104 Ibid., p. 169.

105 For example, John R. Walsh considers Yunus' environment to be primitive. He asserts that Sufi orders are nothing but "the indigenous religious beliefs and sentiments of the area asserting themselves under the guise of Islam.... Death

and resurrection provide the conceptual framework for the thought of most primitive agricultural communities, and in centering his message about these two ideas, Yunus penetrated to the most intimate depths of the mind and the heart of the people he worked among" (Halman, p. 122).

106 Gibb, p. 172.

107 Ibid., p. 165.

108 Ibid., p. 166.

109 Ibid.

110 Hilmi Ziya Ülken, *Türkiye'de Çağdaş Düşünce Tarihi* (Istanbul: Ülken, 1992), p. 112.

111 The German scholar Barbara Fleming raises the fact that the work *Majmua-i Latifa,* written for al-Malik al-Ashraf Kaytbay, the sultan of the Mamluks in Egypt, contains poems by Yunus Emre and rightly asks if this makes Yunus Emre a court poet. Barbara Fleming, "Yunus Emre'nin Eserlerinin Metinsel Tarihinin Bazı Yönleri," in *Uluslararası Yunus Emre Sempozyumu Bildirileri* (Proceedings of International Yunus Emre Conference), Ankara, 7–10 October, 1991, (Ankara: AKM Yayını, 1995), p. 357.

112 Ahmet Hamdi Tanpınar, *Yahya Kemal* (Istanbul: Yahya Kemal'i Sevenler Cemiyeti, 1962), pp. 98–100.

113 Köprülü, Fuat, *Türk Edebiyatında İlk Mutasavvıflar* ("The First Mystics in Turkish Literature"), p.1.

114 Ibid., p. 283.

115 Ibid., p. 12.

116 Ibid., p. 5.

117 Some of Yahya Kemal's poems, such as *Sicilya Kızları* are products of this period.

118 Benedict Anderson, *Imagined Communities: The Origin and Spread of Nationalism* (London, New York: Verso, 1991), p. 13.

119 For a discussion of nations and nationalism, including the Turkish case see: Hugh Seton Watson, *Nations and States: An Enquiry into the Origins of Nations and Politics of Nationalism* (Boulder Colorado: Westview Press, 1977), p. 259.

120 Among the interpreters we can count İsmet Zeki Eyuboğlu, *Yunus Emre,* (Istanbul: Geçit, 1991) and some works of Abdülbaki Gölpınarlı, such as *Alevi Bektaşi Nefesleri*, (Istanbul: İnkılap, 1992). See also İlhan Başgöz, *Yunus Emre I, II, III,* (Istanbul: Cumhuriyet, 1999) and Edouardo Roditi and Guzin Dino, *Yunus Emre, the Wandering Fool, Sufi Poems of a Thirteenth Century Turkish Dervish*, (San Francisco: Cadmus editions, 1987) as well as John R. Walsh, *Yunus Emre: A 14th century Turkish Hymnodist,* The Humanist Poetry of Yunus Emre, ed. Talat S. Halman (Bloomington: Indiana University Turkish Studies, 1981), pp. 111–126.

121 Irene Melikoff, *Efsaneden Gerçeğe,* trans. Turan Alptekin (Istanbul: Cumhuriyet, 1998); Ahmet Yaşar Ocak. *Türk Sufiliğine Bakışlar* (Istanbul: İletişim, 1996).

122 İsmet Zeki Eyüboğlu, p. 14.

123 Ibid., p. 34.

124 Ibid., p. 22.

125 Ibid., p. 103.

126 Ibid., p. 70.

127 Ibid., p. 175.

128 Başgöz, I, pp. 28–31.

129 İsmet Zeki Eyüboğlu, p. 42.

130 Ibid., p. 44. For a brief discussion of this hadith see: William C Chittick, *The Sufi Path of Knowledge,* (Albany: SUNY, 1989), p. 391.

131 Başgöz, I, p. 60.

132 Ibid., I, p. 59.

133 İsmet Zeki Eyüboğlu, p. 87.

134 Ibid., p. 95.

135 Ibid., p. 48.

136 Başgöz, I, pp. 100–101.

137 One of the best works on the issue is the recently published book of Asli Sancar, who has researched and written about Ottoman women and the Ottoman family for years. Referring to the contradictions between the Orientalist image of Eastern women and the legacy of Ottoman women in Turkey, Asli Sancar discusses the status and role of women in Ottoman society in the light of historical sources, including European travelers' notes and the Ottoman court records in her book, *Ottoman Women: Myth and Reality*, (New Jersey: The Light Publishing, 2007).

138 İsmet Zeki Eyüboğlu, p. 40.

139 Ibid.

140 Ibid., p. 49.

141 Gölpınarlı, *Yunus Emre ve Tasavvuf*, p. 159.

142 İsmet Zeki Eyüboğlu, p. 32.

143 Ibid., p. 182.

144 Ibid., p. 25.

145 Ibid., p. 39.

146 Ibid., p. 90.

147 Ibid., p. 243.

148 Ibid., p. 24.

149 Ibid., p. 243.

150 Ibid., p. 245.

151 Ibid., p. 19.

152 Ibid., p. 245.

153 Ibid., p. 246.

154 Başgöz, p. 55.

155 İsmet Zeki Eyüboğlu, p. 34.

156 Ibid., p. 103.

157 Ibid., p. 60.

158 Sebahattin Eyüboğlu, *Yunus Emre* (Istanbul: Cem, 1980) [1st edition 1972]; *Yunus Emre and His Mystical Poetry,* Edited by Talat Said Halman (Bloomington: Indiana University Press, 1981); Gönül Alpay, *Yunus Emre'nin Humanizmasının Temelleri*, Uluslararası Yunus Emre Semineri (International Yunus Emre Conference), 6–8 September 1971, Istanbul, (Istanbul: Baha, 1971); Sadi Irmak, *Yunus Emre'nin Humanizması ve Rumi-Yunus İlişkisi*, Uluslararası Yunus Emre Semineri (International Yunus Emre Conference), 6–8 September 1971, Istanbul, (Istanbul: Baha, 1971).

159 Halman, *Yunus Emre and His Mystical Poetry*, pp. 2–3.

160 Alpay, p. 17.

161 Halman, *Yunus Emre and His Mystical Poetry*, p. 4.

162 Ibid.

163 Ibid., p. 7.

164 Sebahattin Eyüboğlu, p. 16.

165 Ibid., p. 7.

166 Ibid.

167 Ibid., p. 51.

168 Halman, *Yunus Emre and His Mystical Poetry*, p. 9.

169 Günay, p. 27.

170 Halman, *Yunus Emre and His Mystical Poetry*, p. 17.

171 Sebahattin Eyüboğlu, p. 9.

172 Toprak, vol. 1, p. 12.

173 Sebahattin Eyüboğlu, p. 10

174 Sebahattin Eyüboğlu, p. 59.

175 Ibid., p. 5.

176 Ibid., p. 12.

177 Ibid., p. 28.

178 Ibid., p. 40.

179 J.Kingley Birge, *Bektashi Order of Dervishes* (London: Luzac, 1965) [1st published in 1937].

180 J. Kingsley Birge, *Yunus Emre, Turkey's Great Poet of the People*, in the Macdonald Presentation Volume, (Princeton: Princeton University, 1933), p. 45.

181 Birge, *Yunus Emre, Turkey's Great Poet of the People*, p. 46.

182 Ibid., p. 54.

183 Ibid., p. 55.

184 The article was published in a presentation volume prepared by a group of scholars working under the direction of Duncan Black MacDonald at the Hartford Theological Seminary and the Kennedy School of Mission.

185 Birge, *Yunus Emre, Turkey's Great Poet of the People*, p. 56.

186 *Yunus Emre, The Wandering Fool: Sufi Poems of a 13th Century Dervish* by Eduardo Roditi and Guzin Dino (San Francisco: Cadmus Editions), 1987.

187 There is no pagination in this book.

188 Feldman, p. 254.

189 *The Drop that Became the Sea* by Kabir Helminski and Refik Algan, (Vermont: Threshold Books, 1989).

190 Helminski, p. 7.

191 Ibid., p. 8.

192 Ibid., p. 13.

193 Suha Faiz, *The City of the Heart, Yunus Emre's Verses of Wisdom and Love,* Tr. by Suha Faiz, Preface by John D. Norton (Massachusetts: Elements, 1992).

194 Grace Martin Smith, *The Poetry of Yunus Emre* (Berkeley, Los Angeles and London: University of California Press, 1993).

195 Smith, p. 3.

196 Annemarie Schimmel, *Mystical Dimensions of Islam* (Chapel Hill: University of North Carolina Press, 1975).

197 Ibid., p. 328.

198 Ibid., p. 332.

199 Ibid., p. 333.

200 Ibid., p. 336.

201 Schimmel does not give any details and only mentions that this type of thing happened in high society. Most probably she is referring to some fictional and very marginal issues presented in the novels of Ahmet Hamdi Tanpınar and Peyami Safa. See Ahmet Hamdi Tanpınar, *Saatleri Ayarlama Enstitüsü* ("The Time Regulation Institute"), (Madison: Turko-Tatar Press, 2003) and Peyami Safa, *Matmazel Noraliyanın Koltuğu,* ("The Armchair of Matmazel Noralia"), (Istanbul: Nebioğlu, 1942).

202 Schimmel, *Mystical Dimensions of Islam,* p. 337.

203 Ibid., p. 338.

204 Melikoff, p. 87; Köprülü, *Türk Edebiyatında İlk Mutasavvıflar* ("The First Mystics in Turkish Literature"), p. 133; Ocak, p. 49.

205 Yunus Emre, II, pp. 48, 100, 155, 176, 260, 381, 395.

206 Karakoç, p. 8-9.

207 Ibid., p. 11.

208 Ibid., p. 18.

209 Ibid., p. 31.

210 Asım Bezirci, *Türk Halk Şiiri* (Istanbul: Say, 1993).

211 Sunullah Arısoy, *Türk Halk Şiiri Antolojisi* (Ankara: Bilgi, 1985).

212 Ali Püsküllüoğlu, *Türk Halk Şiiri* (Ankara: Bilgi, 1975).

213 Birge, J. Kingsley. *Yunus Emre Turkey's Great Poet of the People*, in the Macdonald Presentation Volume, (Princeton: Princeton University, 1933).

214 Mustafa Necati Sepetçioğlu, *Benim Adım Yunus Emre,* 2nd edition, (Istanbul: İrfan, 1998) [1st edition 1990].

215 Emine Işınsu, *Bir Ben Vardır Bende Benden İçeri* (Istanbul: Ötüken, 2002).

216 It is difficult not to disregard the linguistic problems which greatly damage the quality of the novel. I will provide only a few example: "Yunus, yine şaşırakodu, sesi çıkmadı önce." (Işınsu, 77) "Ben doğru ya ben doğru söylüyorum." (Işınsu, 93); "Gitme, Yunus'um n'olursun gitme diye söyleniyordu." (Işınsu, 109); "Yarın sabahın köründe gel." (Işınsu, 245).

217 Işınsu, p. 37.

A Selection of Poems from Yunus Emre's *Divan*

1 According to legend, Geyikli Baba was a *wali* (saint) of the days of Osman Gazi and Orhan Gazi—who passed his time in seclusion in a cave in Bursa with no companions but the wild creatures he tamed, whence his name, Geyikli Baba ("the Deer Father") comes from. In the legends he is also depicted as a *wali*, assisting at the capture of Bursa, mounted on a deer.

2 Balqis was the Queen of Sheba.

3 *Haman* is the title given to the high priest in the cult of Amon and held a rank second to that of the Pharaoh and served as his chief adviser.

4 These are the divinely revealed Scriptures of the Psalms of David, Torah, Gospel, and the Qur'an.

SELECT BIBLIOGRAPHY

A- Works on Yunus Emre

Alpay, Gönül. "Yunus Emre'nin Humanizmasının Temelleri," *Uluslararası Yunus Emre Semineri* ("International Yunus Emre Conference, Fundamentals of Yunus Emre's Humanism"), Istanbul, 6–8 September 1971. Istanbul: Baha, 1971.

Başgöz, İlhan. *Yunus Emre.* 3 vols. Istanbul: Cumhuriyet, 1999.

Bilginer, Recep. *Yunus Emre.* Istanbul: Cem, 1979.

Birge, J.Kingsley. Yunus Emre Turkey's Great Poet of The People, in the *Macdonald Presentation Volume,* Princeton: Princeton University, 1933.

Bozdemir, Mevlut. *Yunus Emre, Message Universel.* Paris: Inalco, 1992.

Ergüven, Abdullah Rıza. *Bütün Yönleriyle Yunus Emre.* Istanbul: Bergin, 2001.

Eyüboğlu, İsmet Zeki. *Yunus Emre, Bir Ozanın İç Evreninde Gezintiler.* Istanbul: Geçit, 1991.

Eyüboğlu, Sebahattin. *Yúnus Emre.* Istanbul: Cem, 1980. (1st edition 1972).

Faiz, Süha. *The City of the Heart, Yunus Emre's Verses of Wisdom and Love.* Preface by John D Norton, Massachusetts: Elements, 1992.

Fleming, Barbara. "Yunus Emre'nin Eserlerinin Metinsel Tarihinin Bazı Yönleri." in *Uluslararası Yunus Emre Sempozyumu Bildirileri* ("Proceedings of International Yunus Emre Conference"). Ankara, 7–10 October, 1991. Ankara: AKM Yayını, 1995.

Gabeskiriia, Sh. V. *Leksika Proizvedeniy Iunusa Emre*, Tbilisi: Izdatelstvo Metsniereba, 1983.

Gölpınarlı, Abdülbaki. *Yunus Emre Divanı.* Istanbul: Remzi, 1943.

_____. *Yunus Emre Risalata'l-Nushiyya ve Dîvân.* Istanbul, 1965.

_____. *Yunus Emre ve Tasavvuf.* Istanbul: Remzi, 1961.

_____. *Menakıb-ı Hacı Bektaş-ı Veli.* Istanbul: İnkılab, 1990.

Güzel, Abdurrahman. *Mutasavvıf Yunus Emre.* Ankara: Kılıç, 1991.

Hafızoğlu, Talip. *Çıktım Erik Dalına.* İzmir: Çağlayan, 1981.

Halman, Talat S. *Yunas Imriyah: Turki da Azim avami shaer.* Islamabad: Ilaqai Saqafati Idarah, 1971.

____. *Poetry of Yunus Emre.* Istanbul: Istanbul Matbaasi, 1972.

____. *Yunus Emre and His Mystical Poetry.* Bloomington: Indiana University Press, 1981.

Helminski, Kabir and Algan, Refik. *The Drop that Became the Sea.* Vermont: Threshold Books, 1989.

Irmak, Sadi. "Yunus Emre'nin Humanizması ve Mevlana–Yunus İlişkisi." *Uluslararası Yunus Emre Semineri* ("International Yunus Emre Conference") Istanbul, 6–8 September 1971, Istanbul: Baha, 1971.

Karakoç, Sezai. *Yunus Emre.* Istanbul: Diriliş, 1965.

Khourshid, Said. *La language de Yunus Emre Contribution A L'Hitoire du Turc pre-Ottoman.* Ankara: Editions Ministere de La Culture, 1991.

Köprülü, Fuat. *Türk Edebiyatında İlk Mutasavvıflar* ("The First Mystics in Turkish Literature"). Ankara: Türk Tarih Kurumu, 1976. (Originally published in Istanbul in 1918).

Kraja, Musa, Alpan, Nexhip P., *Januz Emre, poet dhe educator I madh popullor.* Tirana: Shtepia Botuese Koha, 1999.

Kudelin, Vladimir Borisovich. *Poeziia Iunusa Emre: Kvoprosu o gumanizme v literature srednikh vekov* Moscow: Nauka, 1980.

Masala, Anna. "Adı Güzel Kendi Güzel Muhammed" in *IV. Uluslararası Halk Edebiyatı ve Yunus Emre Semineri,* ("The Fourth International Seminar on Yunus Emre and the Folk Literature") Eskişehir, 11–13 May 1989. Eskişehir: Eskişehir Valiliği Yayınları, 1991.

Pekolcay, A. Necla, and Sevim, Emine. *Yunus Emre'nin Şahsiyeti ve Yunus Emre Şerhleri Yunus Emre'nin Bir Eseriyle İlgili Şerhin Yazmaları.* Ankara: Kültür Bakanlığı, 1991.

Revnakoğlu, Cemalettin, "How and Where Were the Hymns of Yunus Emre Chanted?" In *Yunus Emre, The Great Turkish Mystic.* Ankara: Kültür Bakanlığı, 1991.

Roditi, Eduardo and Dino, Guzin. *Yunus Emre, The Wandering Fool: Sufi Poems of a 13th Century Dervish.* San Francisco: Cadmus Editions, 1987.

Schimmel, Annemarie. *Ausgewahlte Gedischte von Yunus Emre.* Cologne: Onel, 1991.

____. *Wanderungen mit Yunus Emre.* Cologne: Onel, 1989.

Smith, Grace Martin. *The Poetry of Yunus Emre.* Berkeley, Los Angeles and London: University of California Press, 1993.

Tatçı, Mustafa. *Yunus Emre Bibliyografyası*. Ankara: Kültür Bakanlığı, 1988.

Toprak, (Ümit) Burhan. *Yunus Emre Divanı*. Istanbul: Ahmet Halit Kitaphanesi, 1933.

Timurtaş, Faruk Kadri. *Yunus Emre Divanı*. Istanbul: Tercüman, 1972.

Uluçay, Çagatay. *Yunus Emre'nin Mezarı*. Istanbul: Remzi, 1943.

Uysal, Ahmet Edip. *International 1991 Yunus Emre Year of Love*. Ankara: Ministry of Culture, 1991.

Walsh, John R., "Yunus Emre: A 14th century Turkish Hymnodist," in *The Humanist Poetry of Yunus Emre*. Talat S. Halman (ed.), Bloomington: Indiana University Turkish Studies, 1981.

Yunus Emre. *Yunus Emre Divanı*. Mustafa Tatçı (ed.), 2 vols., Ankara: Kültür Bakanlığı, 1990.

Yunus Emre. *Risaletün Nushiyye*. Mustafa Tatçı (ed.), Ankara: Kültür Bakanlığı, 1991.

B- Works on Sufism

Al-Ahri. *Tarikh-i Shaikh Uwais*, edited and translated by J.B.Van Loon. The Hague: Uitgeverij Excelsior, 1954.

Bilgin, A. Azmi. *Ümmi Sinan Divanı*, İnceleme Metin. Ankara: M.E.B., 2000.

Birge, J. Kingley. *Bektashi Order of Dervishes*. London: Luzac, 1965, [1st published in 1937].

Ceylan, Ömür. *Tasavvufi Şiir Şerhleri* ("The Commentaries on Mystical Poems"). Istanbul: Kitabevi, 2000.

Chittick, William C. *The Sufi Path of Knowledge*. Albany: State University of New York Press, 1989.

Erdoğan, Kenan. *Niyazi Mısri: Hayatı, Edebi Kişiliği, Eserleri ve Divanı*, (Edition Critique). Ankara: Akçağ, 1998.

Ergun, Sadettin Nüzhet. *Türk Musikisi Antolojisi*, ("Anthology of Turkish Music"). Istanbul: Rıza Koşgun Matbaası, 1942.

Ergüven, Abdullah Rıza. *Bütün Yönleriyle Yunus Emre*, Istanbul: Bergin, 2001.

Ernst, Carl. *Shambala Guide to Sufism*. Boston: Shambala, 1997.

Eşrefoğlu Rumi. *Eşrefoğlu Rumi Divanı*, İnceleme, Karşılaştırmalı Metin, ed. Mustafa Güneş. Ankara: Dumlupınar Üniversitesi Yayınları, 2000.

Fahreddin Iraqi. *Divine Flashes*. Translated William Chittick and Peter Lamborn Wilson. Preface by Seyyed Husain Nasr. New York: Paulist Press, 1982.

Firdevsi. *Kutbname*, eds: I. Olgun and I. Parmaksızoglu. Ankara: Türk Tarih Kurumu Yayınlari, 1980.

Galin, Müge, *Between East and West, Sufism in the Novels of Dorris Lessing*. Albany: SUNY Press, 1997.

Al-Ghazali, Abu Halid Muhammad ibn Muhammad. Al-Ghazali on the Manners Relating to Eating: Book XI of the Revival of the Religious Sciences; *Kitab Adab al-Akl*; *Ihya' 'Ulum al-Din*, by Denys Johnson Davies. Cambridge: Islamic Texts Society, 2000.

Gölpınarlı, Abdülbaki. *Tasavvuftan Dilimize Geçen Deyimler ve Atasözleri* ("Idioms and Proverbs Originating from Sufism in our Language"). Istanbul: İnkılap ve Aka, 1977.

_____. *Alevi Bektaşi Nefesleri*. Istanbul: İnkılap, 1992.

_____. *Melamilik ve Melamiler*. Istanbul: Gri Yayınevi, 1992.

_____. *Türkiye'de Mezhepler ve Tarikatlar Tarihi*. Istanbul: Gerçek Yayinevi, 1976.

_____. *Velayet-i Hacı Bektaş-ı Veli*. Edited by Abdülbaki Gölpınarlı, Istanbul: İnkılap, 1990.

Hacı Bektaş-ı Veli. *Manzum Velayetnamesi*. Bedri Noyan (ed.), Istanbul: Can, 1996.

Hodgson, Marshall G. S. *Venture of Islam* I, Chicago: University of Chicago Press, 1974.

Holbrook, Victoria Rowe. *The Unreadable Shores of Love, Turkish Modernity and Mystic Romance*. Austin: University of Austin Press, 1994.

Ibn al-Arabi. *Fususa'l Hikam*. English translation by R.W.J. Austin, ("Ibn al-Arabi: The Bezels of Wisdom.") Ramsey, NJ: Paulist Press, 1981.

_____. *Tarjuman al-Ashwaq*. Edited and translated by R. A. Nicholson. *The Tarjuman al Ashwaq: A Collection of Mystical Odes by Muhyiddin ibn al-Arabi*. London: Theosophical Publishing House, 1978.

Ibn Ataillah. *Ibn Ataillah's Sufi Aphorisms* (*Kitab al-Hikam*). Translated with an introduction and notes by Victor Danner, Foreword by Martin Lings. Leiden: E.J.Brill, 1973.

Izutsu, Toshihiko. *A Comparative Study of the Key Philosophical Concepts in Sufism and Taoism*, Ibn Arabi and Lao Tzu, Chuang-Tzu. Tokyo: Keio University, 1966.

Lamoreaux, John J. *The Early Muslim Tradition of Dream Interpretation*. Albany: SUNY, 2002.

Lewis, Franklin. *Rumi: Past and Present, East and West: the Life and Teaching and Poetry of Jalal al Din Rumi*. Oxford, Boston: Oneworld, 2000.

Massignon, Luis. *Essays on the Origin of the Technical Language of Islamic Mysticism*. Translated from the French with an introduction by Benjamin Clark. Foreword by Herbert Mason. Notre Dame, Indiana: University of Notre Dame Press, 1997.

Melikoff, Irene. *Efsaneden Gerçeğe*. Translated from French by Turan Alptekin.Istanbul: Cumhuriyet, 1998.

_____, *et al, Tarihi ve Kültürel Boyutlarıyla Türkiye'de Aleviler, Bektaşiler, Nusayriler* ("Alevites, Bektashis and Nusayris in Turkey with Historical and Cultural Dimensions") Istanbul: Ensar Neşriyat, 1999.

Nickolson, Reynold. *The Mystics of Islam*. London: Routledge, 1970. (First published in 1914).

Ocak, Ahmet Yaşar. *Osmanlı İmparatorluğunda Marjinal Sufilik: Kalenderiler*. Ankara: Türk Tarih Kurumu Basımevi, 1992.

_____. *Kültür Tarihi Kaynagi Olarak Menâkibnâmeler: Metodolojik Bir Yaklaşım*. Ankara: Türk Tarih Kurumu, 1992.

Qushayri, Abd al-Karim Ibn Hawazin. *Sufi Book of Spiritual Ascent* (*al-Risala al-Qushayriya*). Translated by Rabia Harris, edited by Laleh Bakhtiar. Chicago, IL: ABC Group International, 1997.

Schimmel, Annemarie. *I am Wind You are Fire, The Life and Work of Rumi*. Boston: Shambala, 1992.

_____. *Mystical Dimensions of Islam*. Chapel Hill: University of North Carolina Press, 1975.

_____. *The Triumphal Sun, A Study of The Works of Jaladdin Rumi*. London: Fine Book, 1978.

Shah Idris, *The Subtleties of the inimitable Mulla Nasruddin,* London: Octagon, 1973.

Smith, Margaret. *The Life and Work of Rabia and Other Women Mystics in Islam*. Oxford: Oneworld, 1994.

Sutton, Elwell. "Sufism and Pseudo-Sufism," *Islam in the Modern World*, Ed. Denis MacEoin and Ahmad Al-Shahi. New York: St. Martin's, 1983.

Terzioğlu, Derin. "Sufi and Dissent in the Ottoman Empire, Niyazi Mısri 1618–1694" Ph.D. diss., Harvard University, 1999.

Tezeren, Ziver. *Seyyid Aziz Mahmud Hüdai, Hayatı Şahsiyeti, Tarikatı ve Eserleri*. Istanbul: Edebiyat Fakultesi, 1984.

Üftade, *Divan-i Hazret-i Üftade*. Edited by Bursalı Mehmet Tahir. Istanbul: Necm-i İstiklal Matbaası, 1912.

Uluçay, Çağatay. *Yunus Emre'nin Mezarı*. Istanbul: Remzi, 1943.

Walker, Barbara K. and Harold Berson (tr.), *Watermelons, walnuts, and the wisdom of Allah, and other tales of the Hoca*. New York: Parents' Magazine Press, 1967.

Wolper, Ethel Sara. "The Politics and Patronage: Political Change and Construction of Dervish Lodges in Sivas." Muqarnas 12 (1995):39–47.

Yılmaz, Ali. *Şeyhi Süleyman Efendi*, Ankara: Kültür Bakanlığı, 1989.

C- Works on Literary Theory

Auerbach, Eric. *Mimesis, The Representation of Reality in Western Literature*. New York: Doubleday and Anchor, 1957.

Barthes, Roland. *Image, Music, Text*. Essays selected and translated by Stephen Heath. London: Fortana, 1977.

Bassnett, Susan. *Comparative Literature, A Critical Introduction*. Oxford UK, Cambridge USA: Blackwell, 1993.

Eagleton, Terry, *Literary Theory, an Introduction*. Oxford: Blackwell, 1983.

Fish, Stanley. *Is There a Text in This Class: the Authority of Interpretive Communities*. London and Massachuset: Cambridge and Harvard Universities, 1980.

Iser, Wolfgang. *The Act of Reading, A Theory of Aesthetic Response*. Baltimore and London: The Johns Hopkins University Press, 1980 (originally published in 1978).

_____. *Prospecting, From Reader Response Theory to Literary Anthropology*. Baltimore and London: The Johns Hopkins University Press, 1989.

Jauss, Hans Robert. *Aesthetic Experience and Literary Hermeneutics*. Translation from the German by Michael Shaw and introduction by Vlad Godzich. Minneapolis: University of Minnesota Press, 1982.

Kaplan, Charles and William Anderson (ed.). *Criticism, Major Statements*. New York: St. Martin's Press, 1991.

Makaryk, Irena R. (ed.). *Encyclopedia of Contemporary Literary Theory: Approaches, Scholars, and Terms*. Toronto: University of Toronto Press, 1995.

D- Secondary Sources

Anderson, Benedict. *Imagined Communities: The Origin and Spread of Nationalism*. London, New York: Verso, 1991.

Andrews, Walter G. *An Introduction to Ottoman Poetry*. Minneapolis: Bibliotheca Islamica, 1976.

Arı, Ahmet, "Persian Poetry or Poetry in Persian? Thoughts about Formation and Boundaries of Classical Turkish Poetry Custom." Bilig – Journal of Social Sciences of Turkish World, Winter, 2003, 173–203.

Aşık Çelebi. *Meşairu'ş-Şuara*, Faximile edition. G. M. Meredith Oweno, 1971.

Atış, Sarah G. Moment. "The Secular Side of a Sacred Tradition." *The Living Poetry of Yunus Emre and Jelal ed-Din Rum*. University of Michigan.

Barkan, Ömer Lütfi, "Osmanlı İmparatorlugunda Bir İskan ve Kolonizasyon Metodu Olarak Vakıflar ve Temlikler İstila Devirlerinin Kolonizatör Türk Dervişleri ve Zaviyeler," Vakıflar Dergisi, 1942, II, 279–386.

Behar, Cem. *Türk Musikisi Üzerine Denemeler*. Istanbul: Bağlam, 1987.

Beyatlı, Yahya Kemal. *Kendi Gök Kubbemiz*. Istanbul: Istanbul Fetih Cemiyeti, 1997.

Bombacı, Alessio. *The Literature of the Turks*. (Translated by Kathleen R. F. Griffin-Burrill, Edited by Uli Schamiloglu). Madison: Turko-Tatar Press, forthcoming.

Claude Cahen, *Pre-Ottoman Turkey: a general survey of the material and spiritual culture and history c. 1071–1330*; translated from the French [manuscript] by J. Jones-Williams. London, Sidgwick & Jackson, 1968.

Dilçin, Cem. *Örneklerle Şiir Bilgisi*. Ankara: Turk Dil Kurumu, 1995.

Ergun, Sadettin Nüzhet. *Türk Musikisi Antolojisi*, ("Anthology of Turkish Music"). Istanbul: Rıza Koşgun Matbaası, 1942.

Eşrefoğlu Rumi. *Eşrefoğlu Rumi Divanı*, İnceleme, Karşilaştırmalı Metin, Mustafa Güneş (ed.), Ankara: Dumlupınar Üniversitesi Yayınları, 2000.

Ethel Sara Wolper, "Princess Safwat al-Dunya wa al-Din and the Production of Sufi Buildings and Hagiographies in Pre-Ottoman Anatolia," in *Women, Patronage and Self-Representation in Islamic Societies*, edited by D. Fairchild Ruggles, 35–52. Albany: SUNY Press, 2000.

Fazlurrahman. *Islam*, 2nd edition. Chicago: University of Chicago Press, 1979.

Firdevsi. *Kutbname*. I. Olgun and I. Parmaksızoğlu (eds.), Ankara: Türk Tarih Kurumu Yayınlari, 1980.

Gökyay, Orhan Şaik. *Destursuz Bağa Girenler*. Istanbul: Dergah, 1982.

Gökalp, Ziya. *The Principals of Turkism*. [originally published in Turkish as *Türkçülüğün Esasları*] Translated and annotated by Robert Devereux. Leiden: E.J.Brill, 1968.

Heid, Uriel, *Foundations of Turkish Nationalism, The Life and Teaching of Ziya Gökalp*. London: Luzac, 1950.

Helminski, Kabir and Algan, Refik. *The Drop that Became the Sea*. Vermont: Threshold Books, 1989.

Hoca Saadettin, *Tacü't-Tevarih*. Edited by İsmet Parmaksızoğlu. Ankara: Kültür Bakanlığı, 1992.

Hodgson, Marshall G. S. *Venture of Islam*, 2 vols. Chicago: University of Chicago Press, 1974.

Kabaklı, Ahmet. *Türk Edebiyatı*. Istanbul: Türkiye Yayınları, 1968.

Kaplan, Mehmet. *Tevfik Fikret, Devir Şahsiyet Eser*. Istanbul, 1971.

Karaosmanoğlu, Yakup Kadri. *Nur Baba*. Istanbul: Akşam, 1922.

Karpat, Kemal H. *The Politization of Islam*. Oxford: Oxford University Press, 2001.

Kemal, Namık. *Talim-i Edebiyata Dair Risale*, ("Pamphlet on Literary Education") quoted in *Ondokuzuncu Asır Türk Edebiyatı Tarihi* by Ahmet Hamdi Tanpınar. Istanbul: Çağlayan, 1988.

Konyalı, İbrahim Hakkı. *Abideleri ve Kitabeleriyle Konya Tarihi*. Konya: Yeni Kitap Basımevi, 1964.

Köprülü, Fuat, *Demokrasi Yolunda*. The Hauge: Mouton, 1964.

____. *Nasreddin Hoca*. Istanbul: Kanaat Matbaası ve Kütüphanesi, 1918.

____. *Türk Saz Şairleri* ("Turkish Saz Poets.") Ankara: Güven Matbaası, 1962.

Lamoreaux, John J. *The Early Muslim Tradition of Dream Interpretation*. Albany: SUNY, 2002.

Minorski, V. "The Poetry of Shah Ismail I", Bulletin of the School of Oriental and African Studies, University of London, v.10, issue 4, 1942, 1006a–1053.

Nawawi, *An Nawawi's Forty Hadis*, translated by Ezzeddin Ibrahim and Danys Johnson Davis, 3rd edition, Lahore: Ahbab, 1979.

Parla, Taha. *The Social and Political Thought of Ziya Gökalp*. Leiden: E.J.Brill, 1985.

Redhouse Sözlüğü, Yeni Türkçe İngilizce Sözlük. ("Redhouse Dictionary, New Turkish–English Dictionary") Istanbul: Redhouse, 1968.

Rüştü Şardağ, *Buhurizade Mustafa Itri Efendi*. Ankara: Kültür Bakanlığı, 1989.

Safa, Peyami, *Matmazel Noraliyanın Koltuğu*. Istanbul: Nebioğlu, 1942.

Sancar, Aslı, *Ottoman Women: Myth and Reality*. NJ: The Light Publishing, 2007.

Schamiloglu, Uli. "The Rise of the Ottoman Empire: The Black Death in Medieval Anatolia and Its Impact on Turkish Civilization." In Views from the Edge: Essays in Honor of Richard W. Bulliet. New York: Middle East Institute, forthcoming.

Smith, Margaret. *The Life and Work of Rabia and Other Women Mystics in Islam*. Oxford: Oneworld, 1994.

Tanpınar, Ahmet Hamdi. *Clock Setting Institution* [originally published in Turkish as *Saatleri Ayarlama Enstitüsü*] Madison: Turko-Tatar Press, 2003.

____. *Edebiyat Üzerine Makaleler*. Zeynep Kerman (ed.), Istanbul: Dergah, 1977.

____. *19uncu Asır Türk Edebiyatı Tarihi*. Istanbul: Çağlayan, 1988.

____. *Yahya Kemal*. Istanbul: Yahya Kemal'i Sevenler Cemiyeti, 1962.

Tarlan, Ali Nihat. *Mehmet Akif, His Life and Works*. Ankara: Ministry of Culture and Tourism, 1986.

Turan, Osman. *Selçuklular Zamanında Türkiye*, ("Turkey at the Time of Seljukids.") Istanbul: Turan Neşriyat Yurdu, 1971.

Üftade, *Divan-i Hazret-i Üftade* ("Uftade's Diwan"). Bursali Mehmet Tahir (ed.), Istanbul: Necm-i İstiklal Matbaası, 1912.

Ulusal Karşılaştırmalı Edebiyat Semposyumu ("National Symposium of Comparative Literature"), 06–08 December 2001. Eskişehir: Osman Gazi Üniversitesi, 2002.

Wolper, Ethel Sara. "The Politics and Patronage: Political Change and Construction of Dervish Lodges in Sivas." Muqarnas, issue 12, 1995, pp. 39–47.

INDEX

A

B

C

G

H

I

M

N

O

P

Q

R

S

T

U

V

W

Y

Z